Praise for Erin Murphy's Previous Collections

"Erin Murphy is sly, funny, clear-eyed poet who has the confidence to probe the more tender hypocrisies of our culture."
Lee Upton

"These are portraits that examine social and environmental injustice . . . I'm reminded of Levine, Levis, Laux, and Espada. Murphy's poems ask the crucial questions for our time."
Brian Turner

"Alert to the language itself, she is always physically mindful of its meanings, its play of possibilities. Behind the wry humor, there is a decent, sympathetic love for the ordinary stuff of the world."
Eamon Grennan

"Erin Murphy's ingenious demi-sonnets—a poetic form invented by the poet—[are] concentrated bursts of language that feel both spontaneous and precise."
Todd Davis

"These poems pack a powerful punch: they startle and surprise, often with an amusingly deadpan approach."
Aimee Nezhukumatathil

"Erin Murphy combines the cool precision of a scientist and an historian's eye for pattern and detail."
Sue Ellen Thompson

"Sassy domesticity . . . savvy intellect . . . dazzling and transcendent."
Michael Waters

"I love Murphy's elegiac gaze and the fierce way she demands our attention."
Nicole Cooley

"These are poems for all of us, and Murphy is a master of her art."
Shaindel Beers

"Nimble in their concision and music."
Sandra Beasley

"Poetry that refuses to stand still, that embraces tradition even as it finds a way to twist old forms into delightfully new shapes."
James Harms

"Murphy is a poet at the height of her powers."
Le Hinton

"These poems are fluent in the difficult language of joy."
Mihaela Moscaliuc

"Murphy chisels words down to their musical rawness, providing us a poetry so well-wrought it is unforgettable."
James Allen Hall

"Brimming voices rise from these pages with vitality, breathtaking clarity, and sometimes rightful rage."
Julianna Baggott

"Erin Murphy's demi-sonnets come at you fast, with the tone of riddle, and the imagistic, presentational quality of haiku."
John Gallaher

"Unsentimental and unflinching."
Shara McCallum

"Culturally savvy, mordantly ironic, bemused and poignant."
Carolyne Wright

"I found myself gobbling these babies like jellybeans: some are rueful, others wise, yet every one is yummy."
David Kirby

Swoon

Swoon

New & Selected Poems

Erin Murphy

GRAYSON BOOKS
West Hartford, Connecticut
graysonbooks.com

Swoon: New & Selected Poems
Copyright © 2026 by Erin Murphy
Published by Grayson Books
West Hartford, Connecticut
ISBN: 979-8-9985883-6-5
Library of Congress Control Number: 2026905422

Book and Cover Design by Cindy Stewart
Cover Photo: "Super Pink Moon over Juniata Valley" by Peter M. Hopsicker

Contents

SCIENCE OF DESIRE

Itinerary	23
Science of Desire	26
If you're a girl, say, 13 years old	29
A Good Day	30
ZipCodeMan	32
A Case for the Hubble Space Telescope	35
Better Than Sex	37
Not Yet Named	39
Caesura Section	40
Studies	42
Pushcart	44
Birthday Poem	46
Sister Subjunctive	48
The View from Here	49
Theorem	50
The News	51
Confession	52
Descartes's Lover	54
Elegy	57

DISLOCATION AND OTHER THEORIES

City Birds Are Losing Their Songs	61
When I Think of London	63
Covetous	64
Hotel Bar	65
Consumed	67
Inter-	69
After Reading a Wealthy Woman's Confession That She Has Never Changed a Bedsheet	70
Hunting Season	71
Given a Shot	72
Amphibious	73

My Son at 13   74

My Daughter Asks if a Minute is Always a Minute   75

Why Poetry?   76

Hula Dancer   78

Mango Out of Season   79

What The Former Homeowners Left Behind   81

I'm reading a poem in which a woman regrets not having given
    a copy of *Leaves of Grass* to a friend before he died   83

Dislocation Theory   84

TOO MUCH OF THIS WORLD

What Every Poet Should Know About Natural Selection   87

An Appeal to the Poet Before the Reading   88

Lake Effect   89

Does This Poem Make My Butt Look Big?   91

Googling Myself   92

You Have to Believe This   96

A Lesson   99

After Reading a Classified Ad for a Car That Won't Go in
    Reverse   100

They're Making This Poem into a Movie   102

Nicole Kidman Appears in One of My Poems   105

WORD PROBLEMS: DEMI-SONNETS

This Just In   109

Offsprung   109

High-frequency   109

In an Article on Freud, I Misread 'Erratic Detours' as
    'Erotic Detours'   110

Interview   110

Word Problem (1)   110

Mute   111

In the Camps   111

No Wind, No Waves   111

Roots   112

Poem	112
Sea Shells	112
The Dressing Room	113
Learning to Knit	113
Plot	113
Word Problem (2)	114
Theoretically Speaking	114
The Long Marriage	114
Where I Come From	115
Word Problem (3)	115
Free Refills	115
My Turn	116
Constellation	116
E	116

DISTANT GLITTER

Vow	119
Dear *Fringe*	120
Address Book	121
Rock, Paper, Man	122
Eleven to Seven	123
Dear *Winged*	124
Debriefing: A Poem in Parts	125
Three Miners Died Today	129
Dear *Net*	130
Tête	131
At the Academic Conference	132
Ghazal of the Dangling Preposition	133
Dear *Crevice*	134
Person, Place, Thing	135
Nesting Season	136
Fever Fugue	137
Early March	138
After "The Boating Party"	139

Anniversary   140
Dear *Mediate*   141
Stolen   142
The Other Side of Snow   144

ANCILLA
Hand Mit Ringen   147
Alma Mahler, Postnuptial   149
Kant's Manservant   151
Nietzsche's Sister   153
Jane Austen's Letters to Sister Cassandra, Abridged   156
The Other Daughter   157
Cleaning 328 Mickle Street   159
The Lost Letter   161
Poe's Last Letter, Abridged   163
Calamity Jane at the Dime Museum   164
Emma Lazarus's Statue of Liberty Sonnet, Abridged   167
Mother of Invention   168
Facing Manet   170
Galileo's *Sidereal Messenger*, Abridged   172
To Nellie, with Love from the Letter E   173
Origen de Las Dos Fridas   175
Postcards from Ghost Ranch   177

ASSISTED LIVING: DEMI-SONNETS
Reverse Alchemy   183
Landline   183
Generation Stuck   183
Teeth   184
Pulse   184
Lung   184
Good Measure   185
Safety Drill   185
The World Reduced to Fists   185
Exonerated   186

Worth 186

When I Won a Poetry Prize 186

Trick-or-Treat 187

Fall, Central Pennsylvania 187

Small Town 187

Assisted Living 188

TAXONOMIES: DEMI-SONNETS

Taxonomy of Rasps 195

Taxonomy of Smiles 195

Taxonomy of Canals 195

Taxonomy of the Pre-Seatbelt Era 196

Taxonomy of Taxonomies 196

Taxonomy of Dancing 196

Taxonomy of Cell Phones 197

Taxonomy of Churning 197

Taxonomy of Field Trips 197

Taxonomy of Shadows 198

Taxonomy of Endings That Are Actually Beginnings 198

Taxonomy of Shields 198

Taxonomy of Spills 199

Taxonomy of Votes 199

Taxonomy of Recipes 199

Taxonomy of the Border I 200

Taxonomy of the Border II 200

Taxonomy of Quarantine 200

Taxonomy of Google Autocomplete 201

Taxonomy of Overheard Conversations 202

Taxonomy of Emptiness 202

Taxonomy of Moths 202

Taxonomy of Mouths 203

Taxonomy of Physical Markings 203

Taxonomy of Knots 203

Taxonomy of Things I Miss 204

Taxonomy of *Mid-*   204
Taxonomy of Menopause   204
Taxonomy of Turbulence   205
Taxonomy of Mirages   205
Taxonomy of Fairy Tales   205

FLUENT IN BLUE
I-95 Corridor   209
To the Man Who Stole Our Pregnant Dog   213
Among the Beasts   214
Impala   215
Flood   216
Sibilant   218
That First Summer   220
Dear Son   221
Vaughn   222
The Week My Son Leaves Home   224
18-Year-Old Daughter as Runaway Horse   225
Poem for My Children's Friends   226
When One Has Lived a Long Time in a Small Town   229
Sentence   233
Son Mother Blues   235
Dear Rita   236
Hide-and-Seek   238
Yearlings   240
The World is a Scented Handkerchief   242
Once you've seen a bird in your house,   243
Porpoises   245
After/Before   247
Anthimeria   249
Azul   250
The Internet of Things   252

HUMAN RESOURCES
Indigo   255

Rana Plaza   259
The Boys from Atalissa   263
Recall   271
Nothing to Trade   273
HR Erasure: Policy on Manager Responsibilities   275
HR Erasure: Policy on Policy Statements   276
HR Erasure: Policy on Clarity   277
McRant   278
Ike Turner's Obituary   279
Shitshow   281
Elegy for the 30-Year Career   283
In Human Resources   284

HOUSE AS FOUND POEM: DEMI-SONNETS

Audience   287
Body of Work   287
Cento   287
Docupoetics   288
Ekphrasis   288
Found Poem   288
Gerund   289
Haiku   289
Iambic Pentameter   289
Juxtaposition   290
Kinesthesia   290
Literary Criticism   290
Metaphor   291
Near Rhyme   291
Onomatopoeia   291
Process   292
Quatrain   292
Repetition   292
Second Person   293
Tercet   293

Underground Art   293
Vocative   294
White Space   294
X-genre   294
Yawp   295
Zeugma   295
Coda: Ars Poetica   295

Notes   297
Acknowledgments   301
About the Author   305

Science of Desire

Itinerary

When you're having your hip replaced,
decades later, the drug they'll give you—
the one that relieves memory,
not pain—will make you think,
This is what it must have been like
to be born.

They'll name you Charles or Richard
or Margaret or Laura.

You won't find out for years
it took thirty-six hours
and you nearly killed your mother.
Don't expect her to tell you this
exactly. You'll know by the way
she tugs your hair as if to say,
You're beautiful and *You need a haircut*
at the same time. By then
you'll have issues of your own
that will make you flinch
when she tells you about the lump
in her breast. *Anywhere else,*
you'll think, *anywhere else.*

Your father, meanwhile, will be
the same shadow you've always watched
from the backseat as he looks
left, then right, then left again,
or from the hallway as he sits
on the bed's edge, stretching
his socks up to his knees
only to roll them down to his ankles.
When you're his age,
you'll put your son on your lap

and notice the sweater he's wearing,
the one your mother knitted
before she died, before she had
any reason to believe you'd marry.

In the first grade, you'll have
one traumatic experience:
you'll wet yourself at recess,
or walk down a crowded street
and reach up for your mother's hand
only to take hold of a stranger's.
It's why you don't trust yourself,
a therapist or a lover will insist.
During your first sexual experience
you will think, *This is my first
sexual experience*, and nothing else.
You won't know your last is your last.

Someone will die—a cousin,
a friend, a piano teacher.
Later, when you've outlived
most of your friends, and even
some of your friends' children,
people will go the way of lost socks.
They will be vaguely missed.

Over the years, you'll have
intimate conversations with people
whose names escape you.
You'll answer *fine* many times
when you don't mean it.
You'll wonder why the doctors
never told you you'd remember
the sounds: the piercing
of drills, the pounding of marrow.

In London—yes, you will
make it to London—you'll peer
into a closed bookstore and see
the remains of a final celebration:
half-empty bottles of Guinness,
scraps of cheese and bread.
Recovering from the surgery, you'll realize
the burden of business is not unlike
the burden of the body, the weight
of saying, *This is mine.*

Science of Desire

There is a fine
line between causal
and casual.
Her spaghetti strap
hesitates on her
shoulder like
an unanswered
question. He is
thinking *lingerie*
is the perfect
word: *linger*
all dolled up
in French perfume.
Linger with
an attitude.
Linger like the
finger that will
help her silk camisole
make up its mind.
Something more
powerful than
inertia is at work
here, something
more than gravity
itself, as if
Mrs. Fuller's
chalkboard eraser
never smacked
the wall or plunged
to the floor
in a cloud of dust,
as if even now,
decades later,

it's suspended mid-
air in that stale
classroom.

(*Inertia. Inertia.*
He would marry
Inertia. He would
father Inertia.)
The solar system,
too, is still
propelled by some
unspeakable momentum;
the worms continue
to sluice elaborate
threads only to have
them scraped away.
Do they weep?
Did Charlemagne,
after irreparable
damage to his ilk,
have any regrets?
Would the tightrope
walker, paralyzed
from the neck down,
have it any other
way?

Once at the Bronx
Zoo he watched
a snake slide right
out of its skin
without looking back.

He's seen grown men
leave their children.

He's familiar with
the least resilient
of all fibers.
Steamed or pressed,
it can never be reshaped:
silk has no memory.

If you're a girl, say, 13 years old

living in a vinyl-sided townhouse
just like every other vinyl-sided townhouse
in southern suburbia except for the master bath option
where others have a his & hers walk-in closet,
you may have a best friend whose bedroom wall
borders yours so that late at night
when the world is quiet save for the laugh-track
from *Barney Miller* re-runs (*Barf!*)
you can rap . . . *rap-rap-rap* the secret code
that means *Meet me at the window,*
and there with your faces pressed to the screens
talk comes even more freely
than it does in the undiscriminating light
of a summer day when you ride your bikes
to the Safeway to buy a log of Pillsbury
ready-made chocolate chip cookie dough (*Wicked good!*)
to eat raw on the curb out front, forbidden
like the copies of *Cosmopolitan* that teach you
that an ounce of sperm (*Gag!*) has 160 calories,
159 more than the can of lemon-flavored Diet Pepsi
you'll get from the soda machine at the pool
where Corey the lifeguard (*Total 'throb!*) knows you
both by name (*He likes you . . . No, no, no—he likes you!*),
which sends you into a giggling fit until your mother
warns from the hallway and you scurry back
under the sheets and swear that you will
let your own children stay up as late as they want
(*Swear to God!*) because before you've settled
on a butter-cream vinyl model
with the bay window and breakfast nook,
before you've uttered the words
Do you have any idea what time it is, young lady?,
midnight is your other best friend,
your one-way ticket to what comes next.

A Good Day

at Chicken Out means her uniform
is grease-free and pressed when she wakes up
and it's nice outside—but not so nice
that she thinks about the kids at the river
with their six-packs and suntan oil.
A good day means Carl, the manager trainee,
doesn't make her measure each order of fries
and Eddie the cook doesn't try to feel
her up when she empties the trash.
On a good day, his are the only hands
she fears.

When Billy, the other cashier, makes a joke
about her feet being *big as surfboards*,
she has the right retort at the ready on a good day:
something about her shoe size and his I.Q.

Customers say *please, thank-you*,
and *Take your time, I'll wait* on a good day,
and at least one in a suit takes off his sunglasses
when he orders as if to say, *I'm entering your world
and I don't mind.* On a good day she has time
to sit outside on a concrete picnic bench
during her soda break and imagine
that man in the suit swooping down
from the office building next door to carry her away.

Sunburned girls in cut-offs and topless Jeeps
throbbing with rock 'n' roll don't come
to the drive-thru on a good day. And because
they don't come—because, in fact, on this day
only poets have the luxury of boredom—
they can't spin off down the road

of infinite possibilities. They can't leave
in their wake a trail of giggles that say,
Girl, there aren't words for all the things you miss.

ZipCodeMan

You tell him your five digits
and he tells you your town—
any state, any country,
even the moon, if the moon
had a post office, so the people
on this mid-western street corner
toss out numbers like horseshoes:

02859!

Pascoag, Rhode Island,

21911!

Rising Sun, Maryland—
and by the way, Buck's diner serves
the best crabcakes in the state,
he says and I glance over at my brother
who came here for college
a decade or so ago and took
the scenic route to a degree
and to this girl at his side,
the one with scrapbooks
of Europe and a Rubbermaid tub
stocked with craft supplies,
the one who is so different
from my brother who put off
writing his 5th-grade autobiography
until the night before it was due,
watching as my mother and I
skimmed frantically through photo albums,
looking for pictures of him
and finding only a few, second-child

syndrome—all of my parents'
enthusiasm for first teeth and steps and bikes
used up on me, but not, for some reason,
on a wooden door I'd never seen
before, a photo of which was
preserved in a sleeve as if it mattered
to someone, so we glued it on
the last page of his project,
with the line, *And this is the door
to my future*, which struck just
the right corniness nerve in his teacher,
who rewarded him with an A
and all he ever needed to know
about procrastination and letting
women do his work for him,
not that I am thinking about this
now, as my brother calls out
91659, the zip code for the remote
Alaskan village where he and my mother
lived when I chose boarding school
over 60-below temperatures and where
my 5'6" brother hunted bear
and caught salmon and was the tallest
player on his basketball team
and where I, brimming with hormones,
visited once and rode on the back
of a snowmobile driven by an Eskimo
boy named Ronnie who was
handsome enough to make me
want to forget my roommate
and my all-girl classes and the
production of *Hello Dolly* in which
I was to play the teary Ermengarde,
to forget all of that, until my mother
put me back on the plane,
an Eskimo shotgun wedding
not what she had in mind for her

only daughter, who is, at this moment,
thinking that maybe I haven't ever
committed myself to much of anything,
either, too eager to ride whatever
wave came along, not like ZipCodeMan,
so disciplined, so thorough,
even now as he pinches his temples
and squints at my brother, saying
*Not Bethel, not Platinum, not Goodnews
Bay*, unable to name the exact
Alaskan village, population 78,
and feeling like a failure, his life's work
unraveling right in front of
the Friday-night after-dinner crowd,
his bread and butter, while my brother
grins just a little, just enough to show
he's proud to stump up this man who
can tell us so much about where we've been
but knows even less than we do
about where we're going.

A Case for the Hubble Space Telescope

On Thursday, astronomers will crowd into a hotel ballroom in
Washington to discuss when and how NASA should put down one
of its and astronomy's most spectacular successes, the Hubble Space
Telescope. —New York Times, July 27, 2003

It was launched the year I first heard the phrase,
You can't have a great job, a great apartment,
and a great lover all at the same time,
a theory I believed because my man and I
had just moved to the top floor of a farmhouse
where I spent many unemployed hours
admiring the view of the Berkshires
until I finally found work at a college
where the dean was named Dr. Hubbel,
(*e-l*, no relation), who slurped his top teeth
and most certainly was missing
the *lover* part of the equation
since he seemed to get his thrills
from eliminating positions, a fate
some government officials have in mind
for the Hubble telescope, saying it's time
to *put it down*, like Old Yeller
or the shrubs my horticulturist neighbor
told me had *served their purpose*,
which makes me wonder when
we started killing things just because
they've lasted longer than we expected,
and, if that's the way it works, why there are
so many reality shows and poems
about looking out of windows,
things so unlike the Hubble, which,
despite its flawed-mirror birth defect,
is really pulling its load, keeping a steady gaze
like a husband who comes home on time,
outdoing what it was designed to do

in its decade-plus in the sky, which is more than
many of us can say as we make our way
to gray desks or turn keys to dark rooms
or haul our tired bodies onto other bodies,
barely looking one another in the eye,
the only part of the human anatomy
that is the exact same size at birth and at death,
an organ that spends a lifetime learning to see
what needs to be seen.

Better Than Sex

It's not every day
that a veterinarian
gets a call about
a cat swallowing
a condom. It's not
every day that a man
stands naked in his
kitchen saying,
Look, I said 'balloon'
to the receptionist,
but it's not a balloon,
it's a . . . a . . . ribbed
latex Trojan with
spermicidal lubricant.
It's not every day that
a veterinarian has to
put down the phone
because he's laughing
so loudly that the man's
then-girlfriend/
now-wife can hear
him across the room
where she's cradling
the same cat who,
two years from now,
will be banished
to the basement when
the real baby is born.
And it's not every day
that I think about
the time when we had
afternoon trysts
instead of carpools
and late meetings,

or when—after
the condom had *passed*,
as the vet promised—
we lay in bed and laughed
and laughed and laughed
until it felt like we'd
come all over again.

Not Yet Named

It's 7 p.m., snowing, and all the taxis
are taken. Judy, who prefers to be called Judith,
covers me with her red coat.
We must protect the pregnant one,
she says. But this isn't serious snow—
it's more like the animated flakes in the film
we've just seen about Communist China.
Belle, whose husband calls her Corinne,
strikes a cab-hailing pose while Maryke,
who has made her Dutch name more palatable
to Americans, says, *That's right—you are two.*

In the film the narrator's father was mistaken
for a spy because of his Russian name.
When he tried to hang himself,
his son clung to his feet until he fell, gasping but alive.
Belle's daughter, 9, has just read a book
in which a girl dies after jumping
from a bridge. She has more questions
than her mother can answer. As a child
Maryke spent two years in a Japanese prison camp.
She stopped asking questions.

Soon we will give up on a taxi and trudge
around the corner to a restaurant that serves
only *hallal* meat. Judy will explain that the cows
have been blindfolded against the slaughter
of other animals.

Spring will come, then summer,
then you. Then all the things you shouldn't see—
and all the things you should.

Caesura Section

Fetal distress, we're told
and I picture a small, curved boy
sending flares, orange
flares, against a black sky.
I'm gurneyed to the o.r.,
where my husband, all green scrubs
and nervous smiles, holds my hand
as doctors slice into me, not like a pen
scoring a page but like
a dull hunting knife sawing into a tough
leather baseball glove. I feel
a deep tugging, as if this baby
is suction-cupped to my spine. The doctor
is pulling, prying him loose, and I am
thinking of pulling, pulling words
from my younger brother: *b-b-b-bicycle*,
g-g-g-giraffe, until the day
he learned to say, *Fuck you*,
Sis, with no sign of a stutter.
I am thinking, thinking of the angry
woman in the park, the one
who dreams, every night, of her son
sliding right out of her, *a perfect
vaginal birth* . . . am thinking
vaginal is close, too close,
to *virginal—a perfect virginal birth*,
though God, for me, is purely
rhetorical at this point, as in
God, let this be over,
Jesus Christ, are we there yet?
More pulling, more prying
and then a sputter, not like
a baby's cry, but like

an old dot-matrix printer, a long
eh-eh-eh-eeehhhh, eh-eh-eh-eeehhh . . .
and he is fine, pissing
in the doctor's eye, the doctor
who begins to tend me, stitching
my incision that will harden, scar
like a Braille hyphen, punctuating
the before—the after
like that game, the one in which you fuse
two unrelated phrases: *Once upon a time*
heals all wounds.

Studies

In memory of C.J.

Four million Americans have Alzheimer's disease.

You have one father.

The neurons in the victims' brains
contain protein filaments called tangles.

He points to his head and says,
I'm not okay in here.

Those with the least education suffer
the highest rate of the disease.

When the nurse's aide calls him *professor*,
he lifts his head a little and smiles.

In the late stages, they forget that they've forgotten.

You give your father his birthday gift—
a picture of his grandson—
and he says, *This you, I mean,
then you, I mean...I don't remember
what I mean.*

Ultimately, victims' pasts are erased entirely.

You remember Friday night dinners out,
your father proud he could afford
shrimp cocktail all around. You remember
him pitching, pitching, pitching to you
in the backyard, then shrugging
when you turned to the piano.

You remember the way he screamed in a whiskey rage
over your broken bike, then replaced it
the next day, no apologies.

As her disease progressed, the novelist
Iris Murdoch liked to watch *Teletubbies*.

Your father lies awake in a darkened room,
his Yankees cap on his head, his hands
crossed over his chest.

Death, when it comes, is a formality.

Like *please, thank you*
and *I'm sorry*.

Pushcart

My husband and I have a friend
who grew up a Russian Jew in Chicago
in the 1930s, nearly half a century
before the prize named for those real pushcarts
that lined the streets of his childhood.
He remembers peddlers in suspenders,
green and white striped awnings, piles
of fresh produce, bagels, even neckties.

Our friend couldn't come to our Chicago wedding,
so he sent his younger brother in his place.
Nikolai—Nicky—was giving up
decades of hard living to make a go
at being sober. The week after we married,
he invited us to the apartment he shared
with three Chows in the basement
of his mother's house. Tufts of dog hair
clung to the carpet, and he'd covered
the furniture with knitted throws, still tagged
with K-mart prices.

He set out someone else's idea of celebration:
a cheesecake and champagne
served in plastic flutes he had to assemble.
He watched us drink, then insisted we take
the half-full bottle home with our gifts:
two ceramic boxes wrapped only
in the importer's layered cardboard.
One was darker and slightly smaller than the other,
with inlaid mother-of-pearl. They were too similar,
really, to give together, but too different to be a pair.
Later, on the El, we realized none of it
had been for us exactly—we were messengers

charged with carrying back proof of his changed ways
to his married scholar brother.

When no one was looking, Nicky slipped
back into his old life. He died two years later.
By then, his mother in a nursing home,
he'd moved upstairs. Nearly a week
passed before they found him. I'd never heard
of a body rupturing, of organs bursting open
like over-ripe fruit, blood soaking through
mattress and box spring, through wooden floorboards
onto a dining table below.

I think our historian friend knows what it is
to be a poet. Some of us push wobbling carts
full of boiled chick-peas head-first
into bitter wind on an empty Northside street.
Others luck into a square of sun on Greenview Avenue.
Our apples are polished like memories
on a day when the whole city wants to make pie.

Birthday Poem

It's 2 a.m. and I can't remember
the last name of my friend Joy
who died of breast cancer.
I can see her wig, slightly matted,
with the curls she always wanted,
see her holding hands with her daughter
that afternoon we walked to Long Point.
But the name . . . a *W* I think . . . dammit...
Joy, who kicked her drinking husband out
the last month, who interviewed
the local politician (*no sir, tell me*
what you think, not what you think
everyone wants you to think),
who drew a thousand yellow smiley faces
and called it *Portraits of Prozac.*
Walton? Williams? Winston?
I brought her copies of *Vanity Fair* and *People,*
heated a few cans of tomato soup
in her grease-splattered kitchen.
I never took an SOS pad to that backsplash
or made a homemade stew, never
drove her, like her good neighbor did,
to the Grand Canyon, IV trolley in tow.
I just sat with her every few weeks
in that dark bedroom that smelled
of her daughter's new kittens,
picked up her spilled blue pills
from the carpet under her bed and ticked them
one by one into the bottle,
reaching for them the way I'm combing my mind
now for her name: Wilson? Wiggins?
The tattered paisley address book
is gone so I can't look her up

and anyone who knew her is asleep now
so I can't call—and besides,
my stepdaughter is downstairs talking
to a boyfriend an ocean away,
which is how far I feel from late-night
hushed giggles and a phone cord
stretched to the front stoop,
that is how old I am now, old enough
to have forgotten the name of a friend
who died, *died* for God's sake,
not a friend who gave me a ride
to Syracuse one weekend or loaned me
a gown for a college ball.
Her daughter lives with the ex now.
He's remarried and sober, I'm told.
Once when my husband and son
ran out of gas on Route 213,
the new wife picked them up in her red Saab
and took them to Gumpy's Station in Galena.
She seems nice, they said. Dyes her hair.
Gwinner. Joy Gwinner. And her daughter's name
is Hope.

Sister Subjunctive

It should be the name of a flower:
Anorexia, from the Greek *anorexis*,
a leggy variation of the daisy
with soft, yellow perennial petals.

This should have been a letter.
But it was as if the thing that consumed
you were a remote country
where you could not be reached.

Your last meal here should have been
pasta with clams, black olives, hearty
stewed tomatoes, red wine and the pungent prose
of garlic bread. It was water with a rice cake,

thin and brittle like the fists
I should have cupped in my thick palms.

The View from Here

1. Fan

Splayed petals of a proud flower,
schoolgirls twirling within a fence.
My mother waving goodbye, goodbye.
Endless cartwheel, fist unclenched.

2. Basket

Boxy bonnet, congregation of braids,
inconstant vessel. This woman knows
straw's taut narrative by heart:
clasped hands, clasped hands, clasped hands.

3. Clock

Stained dinner plate in the sink,
discus I could never yield to sky.
Stern face of the man I cannot please.
Moral moon, unleavened desire.

Theorem

The shortest distance
between two points
is the split second
before you sneeze,
the smell of sulfur
from a spent match.
It's an arc of sunlight
teasing a kitchen window,
the jolt of a train
stopping mid-track.
It's the echo of a child
called home at dusk,
the line from a song
you think you know.
It's the memory of a girl
unraveling a knot
of sky-blue panties,
a soldier frisking himself
to find if he's been shot.

The News

A man in a gray suit and glasses
saying *technicality* and *never mind.*
And before this, hushed voices
in our kitchen, my friend's mother

telling mine *I don't want to have to
explain 'erection.'* And before this,
running into Lisa Saturday morning
at a downtown department store—

the one with the spiral staircase
and brass elevator doors—where
our mothers keep us apart, saying
we shouldn't speak until after the trial.

And before this, the policeman at my house
with mugshots in a padded blue photo album
like so many on our family room bookshelf.
And before this, finishing her brother's

evening edition paper route as if nothing
has happened, as if a pale naked man
in a red muscle car has not just
called us over and told us to get in,

just get the fuck in NOW. And before this,
believing exhibitionist is a good word—
like something an artist does—
and not even knowing the word *rape.*

And before this, the satisfying *thud*
of each newspaper's tight missile
landing on doorsteps as afternoon sunlight
unravels the loose narrative of leaves.

Confession

> *A woman who called the parents of a missing girl and claimed she might be their long lost daughter was charged Wednesday with committing a cruel hoax.*
> —Associated Press

What can I say about my own family
except that living with foster parents
feels like talking to somebody
who keeps checking his watch.
They weren't cruel, nothing like that.
They fed me plenty and bought me dolls—
not real Barbies but the hollow kind
with the arms and legs that keep
snapping off and getting lost.

I'm not a bad person, really, like when I see
a mother squatting down to take a picture
of her family, I always offer to take it for her.
There's this split second when she gives me
a look like, *What do you want from me?*
But then she hands me the camera—
trusts me with it, you know—
and shows me what button to push.
It's the right thing to do—I mean,
why's there always gotta be somebody left out?

That girl was gone for so long.
Even if they'd found her, she wouldn't be
the same little 6-year-old who went missing
playing hide 'n' seek, anymore than I'm
that girl who played with broken Barbies.
Life kind of chips away at you, you know,
turns you into somebody else
with the same name.

Would it have been so terrible if they'd believed it?
There'd be a parade through downtown
and a barbecue in the park. We'd go
on *The Today Show* for sure because
I've loved Katie Couric ever since her husband died
and she was so strong, like a brave cheerleader.
After all that, we'd settle into visits for birthdays
and Christmas and Easter—I've always wanted
to come from a town where you
get dust on your shoes walking home from church.

Who would have gotten hurt, anyway?
If you'd have heard her daddy's voice,
the way it shook when he said, *Shannon?*,
you'd have told him whatever he needed to hear, too.
I mean, Jesus as my Savior, we're all waiting
for a phone call like that, aren't we? Aren't you?

Descartes's Lover

*When a husband weeps over a dead wife...in spite of this, in his
innermost soul he feels a secret joy.* —René Descartes

What of a father for his daughter?
She was a baby, barely
able to separate her own body

from mine. I remember
the day she discovered her nose:
she twisted it in her fist

as if uncorking a wine bottle
until—coming to accept it—
she patted it like a kitten.

She was your impossibility:
the only time one plus one
equaled one, and you

studied her the way
I've watched you study those
Dutch still-life paintings.

If you could, you'd set right
every teacup precariously
balanced, every spoon, crust

of bread, skull, pheasant,
pear, wine glass. You're troubled
especially by the red brocade

rug that fancies itself a wall,
swallowing the room's
contents—chair, map, vase,

telescope—troubled, too,
by tiny limbs restless
to hold and be held,

by wails which could mean
hunger, a soiled breech, fear.
Sickness. If you had known

her as a small child, perhaps you
would have seen that perfection
can come from things

imperfect. Perhaps you would have
teased her: *I think therefore
I'm a yam, or a ham, or a jar*

*of jam. You think therefore
you'll scram, my little apple
of the earth, if you know what's good.*

You can doubt everything:
the sweetness of honey;
a bee's sting; a pencil

bent in water; the pool
of candle wax from a night
of love; the universe

dancing around Earth,
its sullen partner; the smell
of roses wafting through

your window while you,
at noon, are still
in bed, your meditations

scattered about you
like handkerchiefs
after a night's fever.

But can you deny
a body swollen with you
to a lob-sided circle,

or the womb of sweet earth
that buried our child,
my love?

Elegy

It could have been December that summer
afternoon at the quarry when you
sought out the shallow parts, diving
spread-eagle as if to embrace any sublimely
lying rock. I dealt with your death
for the split second after each dive
until you sprang to the surface, surprised
at your own resilience.

Who knew then that at Christmas
the gravel truck would jut out of the road
when you, swimming in whiskey,
could not avoid it? Who could splice
that August afternoon with one in winter
as if we can interchange our days
like words, as if all of life is water
washing back on itself.

Dislocation and Other Theories

City Birds Are Losing Their Songs

Sirens, car horns, and revved engines
drown out sounds of their own voices,

so birds choose flatter tunes,
become dull cousins to their

country counterparts. So says
my ornithologist friend

who offers the obvious metaphor:
we're all overworked, overtired,

deafened to ourselves. *Sleep*,
we say, *is the new sex*.

But maybe it's not so different
from accents, like the time

my Yankee grandmother
badgered the Southern salesclerk

for yan until I stepped in
to translate: *yarn*. Or maybe

it's like the cold I had last winter
when my voice, husky with congestion,

conjured Lauren Becall.
My nose was running, I coughed

like a cat hacking up a hairball,
but my husband said I sounded

sexy on the phone. It's all
in the reception, I thought,

like reading a poem. We never
own what we think we own.

When I Think of London

I don't think of Big Ben or Tower Bridge
or Kensington Gardens. I think of this
thin median strip in north Harrow,

three blocks from our rented row house
where many days I abandoned half-planned poems
for a walk to town. I'd find myself

stranded on a patch of grass as cars skimmed by
in the rain, always the rain. The traffic island
was like England itself, with nothing more

than a day away, the coasts almost in arms' reach.
Once I timed it: twenty-two minutes to cross the street.
I don't know if it was faith or trust in dumb luck

that propelled me, finally, to the other side,
toward the pulse of *don't walk, don't walk.*
A friend once told me writing a poem

is like taking a journey to the unknown
and bringing back proof that you were there.
Don't walk, don't walk, don't walk. Run.

Covetous

After Eamon Grennan's "Start of March, Connemara"

You ask how the gulls find the right angle in the gale,
how they adapt to the current and let it take them

the way they were going. I could ask the same of you:
how do you find *thumbed* and *wind-scumbled,*

thrusting them together like lost lovers,
letting them glance off each other, polished stones

on our tongues? Or *glitterwings making their mark,*
a dance linguists call the *fricative,*

a word I love because it is what it means,
unlike *palindrome,* which resists mirroring itself

and sends me, instead, to a girl I knew in college,
the one from Glenelg—*g-l-e-n-e-l-g,* the same

forward and back. She had hips that looked good
in boy jeans and a way of making the professor

believe she'd done the reading when she hadn't
even bought the book. Do you see what just happened,

how I started in your lyrical world of shorelines
and wave-peaks and wound up recording

slumber party giggles through a thin wall? Your gulls:
maybe they don't harness the wind after all.

Maybe they give in to each gust and forsake their plans,
having learned long ago to want what they have.

Hotel Bar

After one shot of tequila,
I'll feel the marble-sized scar
on your scalp, the one you received
in a friendly freshman-year brawl.

Two shots and I'll tell you
about Smitty, the night watchman
who let us boarding school girls
smoke Virginia Slims
from dorm-room windows
as long as we bared our breasts.

Give me a beer chaser
and I'll tell you what he said:
Show Smitty some titty,
show Smitty some titty, a mantra
he grunted under a streetlamp,
one hand strumming below
the belt of his blue uniform.

A third shot will get you
a passionate debate
about poetry versus
Sponge Bob Square Pants,
and, if you're lucky,
I'll say *hash-slinging slasher*
without spitting in your face.

I've done four shots only once,
that night in New Orleans
when I brushed lips
with the Creole cabbie
whose mule-drawn buggy

took me for a wild ride
under the Nevilles' yellow moon.

Back then, I was young enough
to mistake my body's loose
intoxicated sway for a swoon.

Consumed

You wanted a *this*
but got a *that*—

asked for a kiss
but got a hat,

a wool knit stocking cap
two sizes too small,

a fist constricting
your pulsing skull.

There's a woman on
the Lower East Side

who's spent her life
trying to find

the long-lost mate
of each puddled glove.

The storage crate
in her basement flat

smells of *eau de dog*.
Think of all the mittens

you've tucked under armpits
to turn a knob.

Think of those rooms
on the other side,

the hot clear soups
you've sipped.

Think of this:
you eat a rich meal

just before bed
and wake up hungry,

the hull of your belly
haunted. Wanting always

leaves you, always
leaves you wanting.

Inter-

Inter-: between, as in my first newspaper interview,
the one with the man who'd come to art late in life,
whose bronze and granite sculptures craned impossibly
from pedestals as if trying to unearth ancient crumbs.
We talked about the lost wax process, the quarry
where he cut his own stones. When I asked about
his wife, he paused, then stepped back half a century
to the night when they were post-war newlyweds
staying in a Midtown Manhattan high-rise hotel.
Let's say it was the 10th floor, three stories above
the fire truck ladder at its tallest. This resourceful soldier
knotted bed sheets, grabbed his bride and climbed
down one level, one and a half, two, and then . . .

and then, in smoky haze between stories, he lost
his grip on her and she fell—
Interrupt, interpret, interstitial. Say it: *interstitial,*
interstitial—feel the way it shushes between your teeth
and tongue. Or *inter,* the word journalists use for *bury.*
As I left, he lifted a wooden base to reveal the secret
counter-weight that let him defy physics. In his dreams
he wasn't the hero poised to catch her on the sidewalk
below. No, sleep gave him the chance to forget
her birthday, to scoff when she took too long
choosing shoes for church, to practice the art
of taking her for granted, letting love slip slowly
between his indifferent fingers.

After Reading a Wealthy Woman's Confession That She Has Never Changed a Bedsheet

I declare myself guilty of not having made,
with these hands they gave me, a broom.
—Pablo Neruda

I have not made a broom.
I have not made a poem

about not making a broom.
I have not made a poem

about the Haitian farmers
forced to eat the seeds

they should plant. Or a poem
about Dominican babies

warmed not by incubators
but reading lamps.

I have not made a poem
about the mother

of my daughter's classmate
who fixes her children

grilled-cheese dinners
with the iron in their room

at the Motel 6. I have made
many beds but fear I have not

made, with these hands
they gave me, a difference.

Hunting Season

In this rural Pennsylvania county, public schools are closed today
to mark the start of hunting season. On the news, men in camouflage

roam the aisles of sporting goods stores, scoping out guns and ammo.
One of my college students passes around a camera-phone shot

of the five-point buck he *bagged* this morning before class.
It looks like a stuffed deer sucked clean of its cotton batting.

Beside him sits a young Black man from Queens. Last weekend,
cops there fired fifty bullets—for no good reason—at an unarmed

bridegroom, also Black. My city student studies the photo, shakes
his head. *Where I come from*, he says, *every day is hunting season.*

Given a Shot

"The 17-year-old senior, who is autistic and usually sits on the bench in a white shirt and black tie, put on a uniform and entered the game . . ." —Associated Press

The boy's first shot missed the basket
by a time zone; so did shot number two.

But then he hit his groove: 3-pointer after 3-pointer
and a 2-pointer with his toe on the line—20 points

in four minutes, a school-record tie.
In back-to-back broadcasts, the evening news

showed the shaky amateur video, so popular
it trumped a segment on a centenarian CEO.

Admit it: you'd watch it, too. But you settle for
re-reading these lines: *20 points in four minutes,*

20 points in four minutes, play, rewind,
play, rewind. How we love dormant brilliance,

the perfect sapphire dulled by time. If only someone
would lift us up, polish us, see us. See us shine.

Amphibious

My daughter wants to take
a framed oil painting to school,

a nude with loose breasts and a belly
ripe as the full moon. Why? *Because*

we're studying frogs, she says,
and it's a frog. I cock my head

to consider the angle of the draped arm
but can't get past the female form.

My daughter, though, is swimming
in amphibians, bringing home

scribbled pictures of tadpoles sprouting
splayed feet. At night, she sleeps

in the bedroom I painted pink,
her shelves lined with confectionary

teapots and cups. By day, she wants
to be her brother when she grows up.

Lately, she's morphed into
a creature who'd rather squirm free

than be held. O, how we see what we
want to see. My daughter, looking at

a nude, sees a frog for show-n-tell.
I look at her and see myself.

My Son at 13

The way instant replay frames a pitch
to second-guess a strike or ball,

my son at thirteen is boy or man,
a judgment call. For years he colored

inside the lines of childhood. Now,
he shuffles down the halls of junior high

with shoulders so wide I recall my friend—
her own son grown and gone—

who declared my house too small. *Boys,*
she said, *grow big and tall and hairy.*

They need space. I see that these days
in furtive telephone calls and the way he turns

What? into a multi-syllabled snarl. How easy
it is to reduce him to some hormonal

animal. Yet, at soccer games he scans
the stands for me each time he scores

or falls, and last week I heard little-boy panic
when he called to ask why I was late

getting home. At thirteen, my son is a poem.

My Daughter Asks if a Minute is Always a Minute

In the news today a man who balked
at paying court-ordered support

killed his four children with a shotgun,
reloading, the paper said, between each

shot. As they waited their turn, did the others
cover their eyes or their ears? *Yes*, I want

to tell my daughter, *a minute is always
a minute*. But sometimes it feels like years.

Why Poetry?

My gen-ed poetry students want to know why:
why they should read poetry, write it, care about it.

I have as many answers as there are snowflakes
outside our classroom window. And I have no answers.

It's late February. We've just read Elinor Wylie's
"Velvet Shoes" in which she compares snow to veils

of white lace. *What's the point?* one student asks.
Others echo. I could say poetry makes us

slow down and take stock of our world.
But their worlds are on fast-forward. They study

the clock above the chalkboard.
Once, in eastern Ohio, I heard a young woman

read her series of pearl-like lyrics. I still
remember a line about lovemaking: *you empty*

the ghost of you into the ghost of me. After
each poem she lifted the page and examined it

askance, as if to ask *Who wrote this?*
It was nerves, no doubt, a way to distance herself

from criticism. But there was something lovely
in the way she twisted her mouth—half smile,

half yawn—as if she'd just been kissed
by a man she knew she shouldn't want.

Why poetry? Outside, wind sweeps up the snow
and heaves it back into clouds, shredding

Wylie's veils to wedding confetti just released
from a bridesmaid's fist. In this parallel universe,

I write a poem for my students. Snow is rising.
I wonder if any of it will stick.

Hula Dancer

She will dislocate her hips. Or maybe they're already dislocated, a kind of double-jointedness, like the suburban girls back East who wrap their heels behind heads in slumber party stunts. There is fury in her rhythm, her belly a dark blur beneath coconut c-cups. More than once a drunk man in an airport aloha shirt has slipped a hotel key in the cinched waist of her grass skirt, slurring a room number in her ear. She drops the keys in the trash with the paper plates from this nightly luau staged by a fair-skinned businessman from Chicago. After the show, she'll change into a tank top and low-rise jeans with a red thong peeking up in back. She'll board the number 8 bus—named, after a decade of *island time* planning, simply *The Bus*—and listen to Ludicrus on her iPod as she makes her way inland to neighborhoods where laundry stretches across apartment balconies. On Monday, her night off, she'll sit with a bottle of Sunny Delight under a line of dishtowels and her father's boxers as the wind picks up, lifting the clothes, bending the palms. And in between the buildings, pulsing low and steady, she'll see the real sun, Victoria's Secret red, right where it belongs.

Mango Out of Season

My son needs one for science class.
A mango. In January. In western Pennsylvania.

Men go? asks the grocery clerk, wrinkling
his pimply brow. *Yes, yes they do,*

I think, but say, *No, mango.* Can I describe it,
he wants to know. I can't. I've had mango slices,

sipped mango smoothies, but never seen
the fruit whole. We search the bins.

I think *What peaches and what penumbras!*
but a mother searching for mangos

does not say such things. She is what she is.
Last month my son spent six days

flushed with fever. I, too, was blurried
by our own little hell. But hell has its rhythms:

thermometer, medicine, ice chips, rest.
He was my little Buddha, *x* equaled *x*.

Even the Chinese factory girls, fresh from
15-hour shifts, giggle and dance in dorms

where they sleep two to a bed, mindful, when
they toss and turn, of each other's cuts and burns.

Once, at a roller rink birthday party, a mother
confessed she *never should have had kids.*

Her twin boys skated by, trying to catch
her eye. There is one lone mango in the store,

small and solid in my palm. I feel the weight.
It is the head of a China doll. It is a hand grenade.

What The Former Homeowners Left Behind

The hemorrhoid suppositories were surely
an oversight, tucked away as they were

in the butter compartment. But the frozen
meals were another story: beef stews,

chicken soup, pasta elbows in tomato sauce,
each plastic container stacked and labeled

with dates and notes: *Enjoy!* and *My mother's
recipe* and *Vinnie's favorite.* Vinnie

was the husband. As we trailed the realtor
on our first tour, Vinnie kept pace

with our shadows, pointing out smoke detectors
and glass inserts for storm doors.

Forced by a bum leg to wait below
as we roamed the second floor, he hollered

comments: *Attic access is through the hall closet!
The ceiling fan has its own switch!*

Their new home would be a condo
the next county over. *No more mowing grass*

or shoveling snow, his wife told us.
She crocheted on the sofa, scolding her husband

to leave us alone. Maybe she thought
our kids were too thin. Or perhaps she heard

us whispering in the cramped kitchen,
laughing when our son said, *That's okay,*

Mom, you never cook anyway. Whatever
the reason, she stocked the freezer

full of hearty foods she'd fixed the bulk
of her married life. Just before

our renovation crew hauled off the avocado
fridge and matching countertops,

we pitched the meals, brick by frozen brick.
We never gave them another thought.

I'm reading a poem in which a woman regrets not having given a copy of *Leaves of Grass* to a friend before he died

and I can't help but think of Bill Clinton giving *Leaves of Grass* to Monica Lewinksy during their affair and how somewhere I read that that gift was more hurtful to Hillary than the phone calls and the cigars and the Oval Office oral sex because Whitman was something they'd shared in their courtship days and while fucking was unfaithful, the book was a betrayal, and I have to say that this rings true because when my friend's husband cheated on her, when I sat with her in Applebee's, handing her my soggy cocktail napkins to blow her nose, she was most upset about the fact that her husband had taken the other woman to the movies, a fact she kept repeating—*He took <u>her</u> to the movies, he took her to the <u>movies</u>*—because in their 12 years of marriage, she could tally on one hand the films they'd seen—one of which, she said, did not even count since it was a stupid thriller he was willing to see only because his second cousin played an extra in a boxing match crowd scene. No matter how many times she asked, his answer was always the same: *I'm not paying ten bucks a ticket when we can rent it for less than five*, a deficiency my friend dwelled on, ignoring, it seemed, the explicit emails she'd found, one of which detailed certain rompings in the back of my friend's new minivan after her husband had dropped her at the airport to visit her sick mother— her sick *mother*!!!—and while it's Freud, not Whitman, who writes about transference, I can't help but wonder what Whitman, with his hard-bodied boys, really knew about grieving, and I'm not thinking of the formal, ritualized kind of grief—Lincoln and the lilacs, the widow whose husband's body is *dripping and drown'd*—but the slow grinding freelanced kind of grief, nomadic grief without a home, unpunctuated grief that sprawls out breathless and barbaric as an untamed poem.

Dislocation Theory

This poem needs a setting,
so let's make it the beach

at dusk when surf turns blue,
lit by the black light

of a college dorm room.
Better yet, let's set this poem

in a Chinese factory where
a teenage crew solders a million

Mardis Gras beads to the hissing
machines' staccato groove.

We could set this poem in the
tiny white pocket scooped

by an avalanche victim awaiting
rescue. There he is, rationing

breaths like syllables in a haiku.
Where are you? Where are you?

Too Much of This World

What Every Poet Should Know About Natural Selection

When the editor
of a prestigious
British journal read
an advance copy
of Charles Darwin's
Origin of Species,
he found the focus
too narrow.
*Write a book
about pigeons,*
he told Darwin.
*Everyone
has an interest
in pigeons.*

An Appeal to the Poet Before the Reading

Tell me how long I have to sit here.
20 minutes? 35? God forbid, an hour?
I mean, are we talking short subway ride
bored, or Catholic funeral mass bored?
Look at the crowd: half of us are here
because we're your friends or family.
The whole back row came for extra credit.
And those proper folks up front
hope the colleague who invited you
will show up for their speakers next month.
Even if by some chance we like you—
a big *if*—we need to plan our pleasure.
Heard of those pills that give you
a four-hour erection? Trust me: leave
the party while it's in full swing.
There can be too much of a good thing.

Lake Effect

1.

On a typical summer day you skip stones
clear out to the bulkhead stanchions where
gregarious gulls sun themselves. But today

surf curses the shore, and Canadian-fed winds
spit sand in your eyes. You don't think *cause*.
You think *ocean*. You think *unfathomable*.

2.

When your daughter was three and a half, she pointed to a tree
across the playground and said *My birthday is that far away.*

3.

How far off
is your idea
of marriage,
its perfect
narrative arc?

4.

Once upon a time you said *Once upon a time.*

You used *then* as a conjunction.

5.

No matter how far you travel
or how hard you squint,
you're always twelve miles

from the horizon. *Horizon,*
from *horos: boundary.*

6.

Arctic air.
Warm water.
Evaporation.
Condensation.
Snow.
Snow.

7.

Once upon a time you heard a visiting novelist read a chapter
about—well, to be honest, you don't remember what it was about,
but there was a man and a dog and one variety of existential angst
or another. After the applause and before the female college students
in short skirts lined up to have him sign their books, the author took
questions. A boy, maybe ten years old, maybe the child of a faculty
member, raised his hand and asked *What happened to the dog?*
Chorus of amused laughter: how sweet, how quaint, his concern for
closure.

Does This Poem Make My Butt Look Big?

Maybe these words   are

  too loose

 dimply and jiggling like cellulite

like my friend's *hind parts*

  that can't keep

up with her girls' *bird legs*   Maybe

  these words

 need a girdle some wonder garment

squeezing everything

  in its place form-fitting and

 corset-tight as a quatrain

something invented by   and for

  a man.

Googling Myself

It sounds like something
Pee Wee Herman would be
arrested for, I think as I
type my name and find five pages
on the 70s child TV star
who could wiggle her nose
to make a teddy bear
float across the room,
the one who is now featured
on Erin Murphy posters,
T-shirts, and trading cards,
while I'm the Erin Murphy
on page six, the one with
two poems in an online journal
no one has ever heard of,
or page one if you search
for *Erin Murphy, Poet*,
though I fear I'm even losing ground
there, based on a phone call
I received at a poetry conference
when the voice on the other end
said *Hey Erin, it's Stan*,
which made me think
Stan . . . Stan . . . Stan . . .,
my mental search engine
returning two hits—
Stan Plumly the poet,
whom I'd met just once,
years ago, and Stan the custodian
at my elementary school,
the one who had
Stan the Man decaled
on the back of his jacked-up

Plymouth Fury—neither of which
was the Stan on the line,
who, it turned out,
was the college buddy
of another Erin Murphy—
another Erin Murphy, Poet!—
who was not only
attending the conference
but also staying in my hotel,
which made me think
I should have taken
an exotic middle name,
the way Catherine Jones
added Zeta, though I don't
envy her, especially since
I read that she has
new bath towels delivered
every week and then
throws the old ones away—
a little luxury I allow myself,
she told the reporter—
and even this
computation-challenged
Erin Murphy, Poet,
can do that math:
a dozen towels
times 52 weeks
equals 624 towels a year,
a landfill mountain of rich
Egyptian cotton terry cloth,
the kind I had at a posh hotel
(conference rate) in San Francisco
where the staff greeted me
at check-in, cheering
Here she is! Here she is!
until they realized I was not
Erin Murphy, former child star,

who had been a guest
that week and who had
checked out earlier that day,
much to the disappointment
of the clerks and to me,
as I would have enjoyed
chatting with her over coffee
in the hotel lounge,
telling her about the carpool
in second grade, how the smell
of Rachel Hoster's
tuna sandwich mixed with
her mother's perfume
made me so sick that I'd
channel my inner Tabitha
and press my nose
and pretend to make them
disappear, a story
that would give us
both a good laugh,
though we'd know
we could never be close
because you can't be friends
with someone who shares
your name, which I can prove
because my new neighbor
is another Erin and when I
walk out to check my mail
as she's washing her car,
I say *Hi Erin*,
and she says *Hi Erin*,
and it's just too weird,
weirder even than the fact
that Erin's live-in boyfriend
is named Andy, the same name
as the man across the street
who is married to Jamie,

which is the name of the dog
of another neighbor,
which makes me feel
as if this is one giant
Venn Diagram of identity,
which I mention not only
to prove to Mrs. Bryan
that I did pay attention
in 8th-grade algebra,
but also to get you to look
closely at the googol—
yes, *googol*, not *Google*—
of microscopic dots
swimming frantically
in the Venn's *union*,
the shaded center
otherwise known as
the gray area.

You Have to Believe This

because it's true, even the part about driving in the car
    with my son, Nathan, and listening
        to a lyric by Adam Duritz of the Counting Crows
        which we are doing because I'm going

to a Counting Crows concert next month even though
    I hate concerts, actually fell asleep at a Neil Young concert once,
        which is probably some kind of sacrilege somewhere,
            though I suspect Neil Young has fallen asleep himself

at one or two of his own shows, but anyway,
    the Counting Crows are coming to the little college
        where I teach writing—poems and stories, that is,
            not the difference between *affect* and *effect*—and so

it won't be like a *concert* concert, it will be
    like me . . . and a bunch of my students, in which case
        I really should know some of the songs, so
            Nathan and I are listening to *Mr. Jones*

and I ask him about the lyric *when everybody*
    loves me, I will never be lonely and whether or not
        he thinks it's true, and Nathan, drawing on his
            seven years of wisdom, says *no, because they might*

just love you because you're good at sports or something
    not because they love you for you, and I agree and then—
        AND THIS IS THE PART YOU WON'T BELIEVE,
        BUT I HAVE WITNESSES, I SWEAR—

Two days later I'm sitting in a Baltimore restaurant with my mother
and my daughter, Molly, in her highchair with her wild curls
that she gets from both her mom and dad, when
this woman with straight straight blonde blonde hair

and white white skin and pale, I'm talking *translucent*, eyes,
comes up and says *you're 'mumble mumble,'* not like
a question but like a defiant declaration and I say no
because whatever name it is, I know it's not mine

and she keeps standing and staring and says
yes, you're 'mumble mumble,' Adam Duritz's girlfriend
(see, I TOLD you you wouldn't believe me)
and that's his daughter Eden, and now she is pointing

at my Molly who is indeed perfect in every way
but is NOT Eden, though her hair does look like
Adam Duritz's crazy mane, especially after riding in a carseat
all morning, but even after I say so to this strange woman,

she doesn't believe me and she stares and gets this
hollow look like she's done too many. . . concerts,
and so finally we have to get the manager involved
and she's escorted out the front and we're whisked out

the back with a special little tin of mints because
the staff feels bad and has to give us something
and meanwhile I'm explaining to my mother
who Adam Duritz is because she's never heard of him

or the Counting Crows and, in fact, hasn't really
registered the name of any new musical group
since Diana Ross and the Supremes, and then
we drive home, a little unsettled yet amused,

to pick up Nathan who needs a haircut, even though
   he somehow got straight hair despite his genes
      so we go to what we call the Hair Butchery
         where we see a teenage boy looking

a little sad, maybe because of his short short
   haircut, maybe because he's a teenage boy,
      and then he scrunches up his nose and asks *aren't you . . .*
         aren't you the Poetry Lady who came into

my 4th grade class and taught us to write poems,
   and I say, *Yes, yes I am,* happier than usual
      to be recognized for who I really am
         and I, remembering him, say

and you're the boy who knows all about sharks
   and you wrote a poem about how sharks
      have to keep swimming or they'll die
         and if you rub them the wrong way, their flesh

will cut you and the boy, who is now 13,
   it turns out, smiles because he is happy, too,
      to be remembered and known and maybe
         even a little loved.

A Lesson

My Russian friend is learning English.
She's not used to definite articles,
keeps mixing them up or leaving them

out. In cafés she orders *the* coffee,
asks me to pass *a* salt.
Soon I'm confused myself:

You are *a* love of my life, I whisper
in my husband's ear. At cocktail parties
I tell my poet friends I'm writing

the poem. They scoff, then stare
in silence. I can't decide
if they are aghast or *the* ghast.

After Reading a Classified Ad for a Car That Won't Go in Reverse

Think of the metaphysics of it,
only going forward. And imagine
how you'd have to plan a day,
always parking in the back

of the supermarket lot where you
could pull ahead to a facing space,
or perhaps never stopping at all,
going to drive-thrus then looping back

like Columbus set on proving the city
round. In my dream, there is
a geyser rising under my house.
The foundation wedges itself up

like a giant loose screw
and everything begins to flow
backwards: the car in the driveway,
tiny sandbox toys—plastic tractors,

red buckets, Wiffle balls—
heating oil and water from the pipes,
all the symbols of my overstuffed
suburban life tumbling in slow motion

back toward some unknown source.
In another classified ad, someone
is willing to pay $20 for an 80s-era
Burger King kid's meal prize,

a dinosaur that *must have working wings*.
Man, I think, we live in a crazy
custom-order world and I'm afraid
I know exactly what I want.

They're Making This Poem into a Movie

and it starts with a close-up of a Bear Island
sign, and just when you're starting
to picture me (or Nicole Kidman as me)
in camouflage, stalking a grizzly,
or, even better, huddled by the fire
in a log cabin with a stew simmering
on the stove, the camera pans out
to a wide angle and this Bear Island
turns out to be a median strip in Bear, Delaware,
and I'm sitting in the waiting area
of a tire dealership where a guy named Steve
convinces me to go with the Regatta 2
which promises a quiet ride
and excellent wet-road traction
for $60 more than I'd planned to spend,
which, Steve tells me, is only $3 a year per tire more,
and I trust him on this (and here's where
the voice-over kicks in) because
I'm too lazy to do the math and because
I'm impressed that he can say *wet-road traction*
without sounding like Barbara Walters
(try it three times fast: *wet-road traction,*
wet-road traction, wet-road traction...see?) and besides,
I was hoping to be in the library today,
not inhaling rubber fumes and listening
to *Scooby-Doo* re-runs and just think—
if I'd gone to the library, you could be experiencing
a poem-movie about Hegel or Matisse,
heck, even Michener would be better
than Michelin (or Michener on Michelin:
a truly tiresome epic with an 85,000-word warranty),
yes the library is where I'd be now, even though,
as I'm sure you'll be relieved to hear, I'm not the least bit

constipated, which can't be a total non sequitur
for you, as I'm sure I'm not the only one
for whom the smell of musty old books
combined with recirculated air conditioning
works better than a prescription laxative—
I mean, do not pass go, do not collect $200,
send me straight to the library bathroom,
a place where I spent quite a bit of time
in graduate school when I pretty much survived
on cheese from visiting writer receptions,
enough to make anybody's system turn to sludge,
and speaking of that library,
let me tell you about that prime example
of an architectural disaster, that brick skyscraper
in the center of campus that looked like
it was giving the finger to the rest of Western Massachusetts,
that giant phallus designed by a man
(had to be) who forgot to take into account
the weight of the books so that one by one
the bricks started popping out of the sides
and falling like Looney Tunes anvils
onto the walkways below until the university
closed off the top six stories and built
a chain-link fence around the perimeter,
which made me cross my fingers in hopes
that the physicist who calculated a safe circumference
was more accurate than the architect,
which reminds me of a student I had back then
who grew up in Boston and wrote
that she wanted to be an *akitek*—A-K-I-T-E-K—
when she grew up (I'm thinking Reese Witherspoon
for her part), and I figure even that girl
would have done a better job on the library,
a building I think of often because,
frankly, I'm jealous of anyone who can fuck up
on such a large, I'm talking massive scale,
as I work on little poems that will never

be sued for amputating the wrong stanza,
never be sold for movie rights, never be the reason
some union production assistant gets to
stand at the craft service cart next to
Nicole Kidman and text message his brother
that she's not nearly as hot as she looks on screen,
which is a shame, really, I mean,
I want my poems to matter that much,
so much that if you hated this poem
you'd want to sue me, yes, sue me...I want you
to sue me, I do—I want you to put this poem down
right now and find yourself a lawyer,
tell her about your pain and suffering,
demand damages, I mean you endured
line after line about bowel movements,
for god's sake, and don't forget to tell her
I used the word *fuck*—twice now—
and here's a few more: *fuck fuck fuck fuck fuck*,
I'll give you all the fucks you want
just to get somebody—*anybody*—to give one.

Nicole Kidman Appears in One of My Poems

and it occurs to me that one fine day,
if I'm lucky enough to live that long,
I'll be giving a poetry reading at a cafe or library
and mention her name, only to look out
at a crowd of blank faces, to whom I'll say,
Oh, you're too young, the way my mother-in-law
will mention Veronica Lake, then add,
Oh, she's before your time, darling,
when the truth is, I'm barely old enough
to know anyone who uses the word *darling*
besides movie stars like Elizabeth Taylor
whose new perfume commercial shows her
watching a young Elizabeth Taylor movie,
which is creepy, when you think about it,
all of this representation building up like
years' worth of thick make-up or the mountains
of statistics we hear on the news, the latest of which
indicates that only 43% of today's population
was alive when JFK was assassinated,
a number that's a bit misleading since some
of us were babies gurgling in play pens
we'd now call unsafe, the slats wide enough
to trap an infant's head like the stocks
at Colonial Williamsburg, where everything
is as old as I felt when my stepdaughters
needed a name for their new Pekingese puppy
and I suggested Dionne Warwick—since
that's what the dog's scrunched up face looked like
to me—and my stepdaughters said,
You mean the Psychic Hotline lady? because
that's who she was to them, not a singer
but the seer who'd tell you your fortune at 2 a.m.
for $3.99 a minute, which was more than I was paid
when I returned to teach at my alma mater

in my late 20s and, assuming my students—
the ones who thought the Depression was the time
before Prozac—would think I was young and hip,
told them my graduation year, to which they replied,
Oh my God, Oh my God, which made me realize
it's all relative, or, as my junior-high best friend
and I malapropped, *It's all relevant*, which,
in a way, is true, except when it isn't,
like when someone asks, *Who's JFK?*
or (gasp!) *What's a poetry reading?*

Word Problems: Demi-Sonnets

This Just In

The breaking news . . .
is there's no breaking news.
No one died. There were no fires
or bribes or lies. No buildings
exploded or imploded. No one
voted. Nothing happened today.
It's a disaster. Let us pray.

Offsprung

Your children don't choose you.
They usually don't want you
to die. They fall in love with
not needing you. They wear
dark glasses so they can study
the horizon when you think
they're looking you in the eye.

High-frequency

In the land of high-frequency beeps,
cell phones chirp for messages, missed calls.
Coffee makers beep once for on, twice for off.
Microwaves, laptops, clocks, cars locked
and unlocked: beep, beep, beep, beep, beeeeep.
Beeps for convenience, beeps to keep us
from harm. Who is not alarmed?

In an Article on Freud, I Misread 'Erratic Detours' as 'Erotic Detours'

On Libidinal Lane, everyone swallows
jokes about joy rides and burning
rubber. Cherry-red signs say *Stop*
on one side, *Don't* on the other. There are
miles of soft shoulders ahead. Don't think
about how late you are for work.
Don't think about your mother.

Interview

The man being interviewed says
his greatest weakness is he has no
skills. He can't type or file. He's not
a people person. Or a plant person.
He gestures to the mustard on his shirt:
Plus, I'm a slob. The position is VP
of Honesty. We offer him the job.

Word Problem (1)

If a vehicle is traveling 55 miles per hour
on a 400-mile trip, and a 4th-grade girl
with a tear-shaped mole on her left cheek
factors in two rest stops and a lunch break
on a rickety fishing pier, how many
hours will it take her to realize she's
an artist, not an idiot? How many years?

Mute

The boy refuses to speak.
His mother swears he's a river
of words at home. Elsewhere,
he nods and smiles and mimes,
flashing acrobatic eyes. *Speak*,
we say. *Give*. He longs to be
a vessel. We demand a sieve.

In the Camps

Mothers were told to fold
their children's clothes
as if they would return for them.
Pile after neat pile of empire
dresses, collared shirts,
woolen britches—the jaundiced
sky their only witness.

No Wind, No Waves
—Chinese proverb

There's no wave without wind,
no after without before,
no curse without precursor,
no filthy rich without dirt poor.
There's no drought without thirst,
no score without a test. There's no
no without a longed-for yes.

Roots

Spatula, from the Latin:
spatha, flat tool or weapon
for turning, hurling, prying.
Tongue, from *dnghwa*,
Proto-Indo-European.
Tongue: flat tool or weapon
for tasting, talking, lying.

Poem

Sometimes a poem is a poem,
a hot-air balloon lifting you
above the river that curls like
a question mark. Other times,
a poem is a bridge. You cross
at night. Bats pretend to be birds.
You can't tell dark from dark.

Sea Shells

Collecting sea shells, you don't stop
until your hands and pockets are full.
You find the thick ear of an oyster valve,
the whisper of a chipped whelk.
Which ones are dull, which glisten?
You rinse each shell, hold it against
the sun. It's what comes next—revision.

The Dressing Room

Pierre Bonnard, oil on canvas, 1914

The woman sits on the bed,
a black dog curled beside her
like a comma. All around, life's clutter:
mauve table skirt, golden dressing
gown, pitcher & bowl. Framed
in the mirror, the woman is her own
painting, her own tableau.

Learning to Knit

I am learning to knit
you a narrative. Knit one,
purl two you a story.
It will help ward off
the lyric chill. Take it
to bed. Wrap yourself up
in he said, she said.

Plot

The main character marries
the wrong man. She moves
from room to room, from
city to seaside. In between:
corseted rage, lies. It's true
she learns from her mistakes
too late. It's true she dies.

Word Problem (2)

A book distributor orders 210 copies
of a novel. The copies are evenly
distributed to 15 stores. Each book
sells for 12 dollars, the cost of three lattes
or a fifth of gin. The book took eight years
to write. How many copies will the author
find next fall in the remainder bin?

Theoretically Speaking

after John Koethe

The theories have all been formulated,
the songs all written and sung.
The bar tabs have all been tabulated,
the actors cast, the doorbells rung.
There's no question left to ask,
no place left to invade. There's no
love. All the love's been made.

The Long Marriage

They've been married 57 years.
Almost 58. He can't get enough of her
corn casserole. She likes how he looks
in suspenders. Only one of their kids calls
for money. They don't worry much
about the rest. Their secret? *No secret,*
she says. *We like each other, I guess.*

Where I Come From

Where I come from, the air is still as glue
and hot as the breath of a dog who wants
something from you. Girls order desserts
they like least so they won't overeat and take
each step as if walking in stockinged feet
on streets of glass. Where I come from, if you
want something—anything—be afraid to ask.

Word Problem (3)

Monica runs an errand for her neighbor,
Mrs. Sandoval. She skips to the store
and buys 12 pieces of fruit. She purchases
three times as many oranges as bananas.
How many fist-sized oranges does Monica
hurl at the man on the sidewalk who
grabs her pigtail and hisses *Pretty girl?*

Free Refills

Because I was born before free refills,
I mastered the art of rationing a single drink
throughout a meal, leaving a swig
to flush down the final bite. Pity the sibling
who stole a sip. Curse the tipped glass,
the cup under-filled. Curse myself for doling
out poems, whole days spilled.

My Turn

When it's my turn, I won't go
quietly. I will claw and bite, curl
my toes into the floor. Once I left
a candy bar in the hot car. I oozed
the chocolate lava into my mouth,
licked my fingers and the wrapper
clean. Still, I wanted more.

Constellation

I took an evening astronomy class
with my father when the only safe
topic was the sky. I have lobbed
the words *I love you* with no one
there to catch them on the other side.
I owe three people apologies.
Two of them know why.

E

It's true we're drawn to things
whose names begin with the same letter
as our own. I, for one, love the elephant,
lumbering elegy to an earlier era. And eggs,
emergency-red exit signs, the human ear.
I love especially ephemera's epitome: the Etch-
a-Sketch. Shake me up. Watch me disappear.

Distant Glitter

Vow

Somewhere, a child pretends to sleep—
eyelids fluttering in the nightlight's

flannel glow—while an office worker
feigns wakefulness in his cubicle,

startling at each chirping phone.
Someone is catching a ball.

Someone is catching her breath.
Someone, somewhere is lingering

between this world and the next.
Things come and go. Things

go and go. Because of the ocean,
the sky is blue. Because of death,

we learn how to live. Or do we?
Someone, somewhere is saying *I do*.

Dear *Fringe*

Jangle on a flapper
girl's dress, yes, but also

her bangs and lashes.
Grass in the pasture

not yet grazed or flattened.
Shop talk, small talk.

Ropy belly fur
on a river-loving dog.

A marginal student's
marginal doodles. Tears.

The line of plastic caps
my grandmother twisted

onto toothpaste tubes
for forty hours a week

and forty years.
The receiving line:

handshake, handshake,
handshake, kiss. This.

Address Book

Their new house,

her new name,

his new wife.

Hearse black

permanent marker

for those who've moved

on from this life.

Rock, Paper, Man

Scissors cut paper.
Paper obscures rock.
Rock smashes scissors.

Man smashes glass.
Glass obscures words.
Words cut man.

Eleven to Seven

At midnight her work was just beginning:
churn of conveyor belt, grind and crank

of body and machine. That last year
she stood on the gel mat I sent for Christmas,
its rubber taffy cushioning her joints until

she stepped out into the blinking dawn.
Third shift, blurred rift

between black and white. So many ways
to block out light: curtains, masks, pills.

So many bills. Even on days off,
at midnight her work was just beginning.

She stepped out into the blinking dawn,
ferrying my mother to school, then returning
to fold and starch the clothes

she'd hung under watchful stars, pinning
hopes not on her own future but on ours.

Dear *Winged*

The opposite of water,
lighter than dried ink, thinner
than a garlic bulb's paper

skin. The thought before
we think, echo set adrift,
white silk ribbon unraveling

on an unexpected gift.
Cacophony of moths. Fragile
as egg shells—and as strong.

The way we leave this
place. The only grace note
in our only song.

Debriefing: A Poem in Parts

I. My Left Leg

My left leg struts up the street
in search of a full-bodied
cup of cardamom coffee in a cafe

where men in snug trousers talk
with their eyebrows. My left leg
lingers by grilled kababs and blood

red pomegranate juice, by vendors
unscrolling grates for late-night
shoppers. On a candle-lit veranda

overlooking the Tigris, you'll find
my leg engaged in a cutthroat
game of Backgammon

or caught up in the rapid-fire
ticks of Domino tiles. My leg
sits in Hurriah Square with lovers

who lick each other's ice cream cones
as if they're kissing. My left leg
has no idea what it's missing.

II. Language Redeployment: *Beach Party*

(n): a task organization charged with facilitating the landing and
movement off the beaches of troops, equipment, and supplies

III. Six Alternative Uses for Tampons

      squeegees for dusty night-vision goggles

      Nerf darts for slow days on rooftop patrol

      ornaments for Christmas cacti

      toys for flea-bitten alley cats

      makeshift spoons for MREs

      plugs for bullet wounds

IV. Language Redeployment: *Early Spring*

(n): an anti-reconnaissance satellite weapon system

V. At the Reading

I am sitting.
I am sitting at a poetry reading.
I am sitting at a poetry reading beside my student.
I am sitting at a poetry reading beside my student, an
    Iraq War veteran.
I am sitting at a poetry reading beside my student, an
    Iraq War veteran who lost his leg.
I am sitting at a poetry reading beside my student, an
    Iraq War veteran who lost his leg,
        and we are listening to another
veteran read his poems about the war.

My student is turning pages in his book, following
    along with each poem.

My student is turning pages in his book, following
    along.
My student is turning pages in his book.
My student is turning pages.
My student is turning.
My student is turning.

Mortar, the poet says.
Mortar, the poet says, and I think of my student.
Mortar, the poet says, and I think of my student
    thinking of his father.
Mortar, the poet says, and I think of my student
    thinking of his father smashing his fist on the
    kitchen table at 2 a.m.

I think of my student. I think of *my*.
I think of what I think is mine, of what is his.
Mortar, the poet says, and I think of how close it is
    to *mortal*.
Mortar, the poet says, and I think of how close it is.

VI. Language Redeployment: *Free Play*

(n): an exercise to test the capabilities of forces under
    wartime conditions

VII. If You Are Reading This

If you are reading this,
I wish I could hit rewind.

If you are reading this,
I guess it was a one-way trip.

If you are reading this,
Mom, don't be sad.

If you are reading this,
Dad, take care of Mom.

If you are reading this,
I have one request: bagpipes

and "Amazing Grace"—
okay, that's two.

If you are reading this,
Jake, you can have my truck

but don't ride the clutch
cuz I'm watching you.

If you are reading this,
it was my time to go.

If you are reading this,
you already know.

Three Miners Died Today

trying to rescue another six.
On the news, apologies from

the surly boss. Such cruel math,
this: the bottom line, the net loss.

Dear *Net*

Hemp honeycomb, nylon nest,
knotted teardrop on the fishing

pier. You are a mesh corset
for the lunch lady's perm

as she scoops waxed beans
on tray after tray, year after year.

Each time I cast you into the void,
you come back empty, loose

as sloughed skin. You are a cradle
of flailing fish, a vessel for water

and grief. Oh, the things you cannot
hold. The things you can't release.

Tête

after an etching by Henri Matisse, ca. 1915

a haiku of hair, eyes,
chin and lips

*

a Quaker meeting, its silence
broken only by those moved to speak

*

a woman's hips glimpsed
through a beige linen dress

*

hint of osprey wings drifting
through the river's gray veil

*

a lover's breathless *oh*—and later,
the *oh* in learning she's been betrayed

At the Academic Conference

I grow tired of the preening
panelists and walk four blocks

to the real zoo. It's February.
The sidewalks are edged

with snow. I shake my own
unruly mane at the male lion

who leaps to his feet and roars,
protecting his pride. In the reptile

house, an alligator snapping turtle
waits for prey with beak agape,

as if the hinges of his mouth
are clogged with rust. Gorillas

rap the glass and vomit a lumpy
pink paste, then lick the concrete

clean. Back at the conference,
all the papers are titled *Look at Me*.

In the hallways, attendees crow
I know, I know, I know, I know,

I know more than you know.
Gorillas rarely vomit in the wild,

a guide explains. They see us
watching them. It's all for show.

Ghazal of the Dangling Preposition

I need someone to sing to, undress with,
shake my ass at, and shower with.

Someone to bitch to, cut calories for,
get pissed off at and make up with.

To hold up and be held by when I'm
down, to see through, to read to and with.

To wax my legs and bikini area for
and make fun of other people with.

Someone to be on top of and beneath,
someone to fall asleep and wake up with.

To wink at across a crowded room,
drink with, talk dirty to, and be flirty with.

Someone to apply Vick's VapoRub to,
schedule colonoscopies for, and floss with.

I need someone to lie to, for, about, with.
Someone to cry to, for, about, with.

Someone to write to, for, about, with.
Someone I'd die for, without, and yes, with.

Dear *Crevice*

Notch in my newborn niece's chin,
same as her father's, brisk flick

of a sculptor's wrist. Pauses—
breath held to hear a child's,

lulls in conversations, marriages, flawed
hearts. Sofa cushions and all

they've taken: coins, toys, keys,
innocence. Skin to be explored:

clavicle, labia, inner thigh.
Or in old age, the tributaries

long ignored by lovers and wash cloths
alike, repositories of brine and rot.

The fissure between everything we wanted
to remember but forgot.

Person, Place, Thing

The day my son learns the word
wheelbarrow, he also learns

hammock. Confusing
the two, he wants to swing

in the wheelbarrow and fill
the hammock with crisp leaves.

When language slipped from
Emerson's grip, he'd substitute

associations: *Give me one
of those things everyone loses*,

he'd say when he needed
an umbrella. We're visiting a farm

in Vermont where rusty tractors
and weathered barns pose like objects

in a still life tableau. My son sees
the ropy sling of a hammock

strung between two trees
and says *Wheelbarrow! Let's sit!*

It's not red or glazed with rain.
Yet so much depends on it.

Nesting Season

for Nathan

That night we licked our plates
clean of *tres leches*, then looked up

to see the local boys in screened darkness.
Wild-armed, they summoned us with

Tortugas! Tortugas! You were four. You
greeted the world with the two-clawed

wave of a tyrannosaur. We scurried across
the road, mindful of motorbikes buzzing by

without headlights. On the playa, the surf
was moonlit amethyst. *Aquí, aquí,* the boys

motioned and so we squatted, made our
breath so small we could hear the mother

sea turtle before we saw her, the hulk of her
body swimming on dry land. Nearly the size

of your baby pool back home, she muscled
prehistoric flippers into sand. Then: stillness.

Then: the first egg, paper-thin, glistening.
My hand on your shoulder said *Patience.*

Your round face said *Wonder.* Then: another egg.
And another. A ritual both new and ancient.

Fever Fugue

I'm not home. I'm out of town.
My daughter calls me
on the phone. She has a fever.
My daughter calls me. I try
to comfort her. I'm out of town.
She says hold on. I hear her
vomiting in the background.
I'm out of town. My daughter
has a fever and calls me
on the phone. The sitter
is downstairs and doesn't know
what's going on. I'm out of town.
My daughter is vomiting.
Get the sitter, I say.
She says hold on. My daughter
calls me on the phone. I try
to comfort her. I sing her a song.
My daughter's sick. I hear her
call me. I'm trying to hold on.

Early March

Yesterday's temperatures
dipped into the teens—today
they'll chug uphill toward forty.

In our yard, islands of snow
form their own ever-shrinking
nations. The TV meteorologist

calls it *roller coaster weather*
and points to an animated
ride hovering over our state.

My daughter takes this
to mean it's the perfect day
for an amusement park,

the perfect day—like every day—
to toss your arms up and scream
till you almost taste your heart.

After "The Boating Party"

My mistake was in devoting myself to art,
instead of having children. —Mary Cassatt

Is the woman gazing at the man
or beyond him? In her eyes, do we see

indifference or a plea for affection?
Is the pink baby milk-fattened

and content or desperate
to wrest free? Is the man teasing

the child with a winsome smirk
or scolding her for squirming? Is the water

blue-green or gray-blue? Did Cassatt
make a mistake? Did I? Did you?

Anniversary

In twenty years, the two of us
have cradled a halo of sighs:
one union, two marriages,
the before, the after, the rift.
The mind and eye,
easily distracted, drift.

/

Easily distracted drift
the mind and eye—
the before, the after, the rift.
One union, two marriages
have cradled a halo of sighs.
In twenty years: the two of us.

Dear *Mediate*

You're the center beam
of a teeter-totter, the place

water goes to seek its own
level. You've learned that

if you want to play God,
you've got to spend time

with the Devil. You shake
hands with men on death row

and the letter-writing women
who find them handsome.

Some days you're the hostage,
other days the ransom.

Stolen

Do you remember the girl
who tucked her thesis

under her arm and planned
to deliver it by bicycle, then

ride until dark in the folds
of the Berkshires? When she

stepped out of the apartment
that smelled of the neighbor's

goulash, she found the garage
sprung open in awe, her ten-speed

gone. So she called the classmate
who was moving, the one whose

flyers featured an old red racer
with hybrid tires, and for thirty-five

bucks she bought the bike
and pedaled three and a half blocks

to the dusty building where
she slipped the package under her

professor's office door. And then
she rode and rode, dipping between

shadows and sun, the May air
cool against her moist face.

I don't recall a word of that
last assignment. I barely remember

what she looked like: skin taut
across bones, a gaze like a song

about to be sung. I barely
remember being so young.

The Other Side of Snow

In college I read a poem
my professor wrote about snow.
What's there to say? I thought.

It's white. It's cold. Flash forward
twenty years to this evening:
dusk casts a lavender shadow

on a field of new snow, a field
almost large enough to hold
all the things I still don't know.

Ancilla

Hand Mit Ringen

> *I have seen my death!*
> —Anna Bertha Röntgen, upon seeing her hand captured by
> her husband, Wilhelm, in the first x-ray

At first you were no different
from the others who frequented
my father's café. Some came

for food and drink; others called
upon Papa to translate their essays
into Latin. But you, it seemed,

had other designs. Your eyes cut
through the bar's din and clatter
to meet mine. When I gave you

my hand, I never meant it
literally, and yet there it is
ring and all, immortalized

in a bony bon voyage. I still
remember that winter evening
in your lab, the heartbeat of

the grandfather clock, wires
and bulbous tubes, the window
a photograph of skeletal trees.

Your colleagues said we'd be
in high fortune if you'd patent
your findings. But you were

never one to take credit.
At the Nobel ceremony, you
slipped out the back door before

they called you to the stage. Nor
did you ever assign blame. I love
the story of your classmate

chalking a caricature of the teacher
on the heating stove. Refusing
to reveal his name, you were

sent out into the cold with no hope
for a degree. But you showed them
all and did what you had to do.

Dear Wilhelm, we have everything
but time. And I don't need an x-ray
to see what's inside of you.

Alma Mahler, Postnuptial

A husband and wife who are both composers: how do you
envisage that? If, at a time when you should be attending to
household duties or fetching me something I urgently needed . . .
if at such a moment you were befallen by 'inspiration': what then?
From now on you have only one profession: to make me happy!
—Gustav Mahler to Alma before they married

Gustav, I composed
myself and became your

bride, swallowing scores
that lay inside me, waiting

to be born. I learned to play
the scales of others'

desires—first yours,
then our daughters',

their cries like crystal
chimes. Yet even

that role wasn't mine
to keep. When little Maria

fell ill, color rushing
from flushed cheeks,

you turned within. And I—
I turned to other men.

What could have been
a feud became, instead,

a fugue. I've given up
my music. I've given up

my name. You treat me
as you treat your

orchestra: like a lion
that must be tamed.

Kant's Manservant

> *Marriage is the reciprocal use of each other's sexual organs.*
> —Immanuel Kant

Sir, a confession: the beef I served
at mealtime today was cut from a cow
killed in anger, not lulled to death

as you prefer. And I was the one
who urged Jachmann to join you
on your walk along the linden trees,

defying boldly your fear of speaking
in open air. It all comes back
to the gold jacket, the one you'd

have me sell, its hue too close
to the sun. Forgive me, sir, but you
could use a little color. The walls,

bare but for the muted engraving
of Rousseau, are blank as the page
you face at your desk each dawn,

bent bird in a nightcap and gown,
still stiff from my pressing.
Sir, what moves you? They would have

married you, both ladies, had you not
stayed so long in the dark room
of your mind. Ending a meal in laughter

will urge your bowels along but won't
bleach your life of desire. Know this:
I will wear the jacket for my wedding, sir,

for my bride-in-waiting who will be
beautiful, simply, objectively beautiful,
dancing the ländler, tucking a yellow curl

behind her ear. And you will grant me
leave for the afternoon. Yes, you will
grant me leave with pay, so that

years from now I will be here
to pour you a pint of claret, to collect
the scattered crumbs that are your words.

Nietzsche's Sister

Man shall be educated for war and woman for the recreation of the warrior. —Friedrich Nietzsche

A nurse, Friedrich.
You were a nurse
in the war, a nurse
with no stomach

for blood. As for
the war of the mind,
let's not forget
whose has gone soft

as our father's:
they found you
plowing the piano
with your elbows,

and before that,
on your knees,
embracing a mare
in the streets of Turin.

Tell me, brother:
if a young girl cries
and no one listens,
does she make

a sound? Not in a house
brimming with women
who serve a boy
named for a king.

When your palm
was scorched from
the batch of matches
you lit to prove

a schoolyard point,
I cried for you.
But now my tears
are a puzzle.

Are we not happy,
you ask, *Are we not?*
It was a *we*
I wanted when I ran

to Bernhard,
to everything you
loathed. You
called me *llama*

and I dipped this
bitterness in honey
and played the part
of mascot. But I

know the likeness
you drew: a llama
sprays spittle
at its rival, coughs

its own fodder
to keep the fight.
Now, with your
right side limp

as the wool britches
mother mended
for you in the evenings,
mark these words:

I will scream
and stomp and kick
and cough and spit:
I will make noise.

Jane Austen's Letters to Sister Cassandra, Abridged

January 1796

I   was   nice.

    I   behaved.

      But   love

  was   cut-up

      silk   gloves

  and   old   paper

hats.   Regret

      is   a   vessel,

  not   a   spinning-wheel.

The   wind   proved

        to   be   my

  future,   delivered   it

      to   me   with

a   sigh.   I   flirt

      with   tears.

    I   write.

The Other Daughter

Mary Wollstonecraft's first child addresses her mother

They knew there was trouble
when the doctor brought puppies
to your breasts to draw milk.

    Stroke the cat. Play with the dog.
    Eat the bread. Drink the milk.

I was a shadow in the hall,
half-sister, step-child to a man
whose indifference stung
more than hate.

    Lay down the knife. Look at the fly.
    See the horse. Shut the door.

In the years since the baby
named for you took your place,
I have grown less sure
about Scandinavia, about
whether the memories are mine
or yours, preserved now
on the study shelf with your lessons.

    Get your book. Hide your face.
    Wipe your nose. Wash your hands.

I still taste the herring,
still see the Swede servants
washing linen in the winter sea,
their hands, cut by ice,
cracked and bleeding.

Why do you cry? Shake hands.
I love you. Kiss me now. Good girl.

It must have been cold,
but I found warmth
in the curve of your neck,
those days before the laudanum,
before the jump from Putney Bridge,
before the midwife and the whispers
and the closed doors, before I had to live
with this girl, hungry as ivy,
always clawing her way elsewhere.

The bird sings. The fire burns.
The cat jumps. The dog runs.

You named me for your friend
who died giving birth.
O, so many parallels, so many
lives running side by side
toward different destinations!

The bird flies. The cow lies down.
The man laughs. The child cries.

I love you, mother.
Kiss me now.
The child dies.

Cleaning 328 Mickle Street

Since you was here, Alma, I have had a friend move in, Mrs. Davis,
strong & hearty & good natured, a widow, young enough, furnishes
me my meals & takes good care.
—Walt Whitman in a letter to Mrs. Alma Johnston, March 4, 1885

It was not for marriage
that I moved in with you,
Mr. Whitman, and not for
peace & quiet, either: the trains
from Camden and factory whistles
rival only the "Star Spangled Banner"
bellowed from your bath.
It was for no such proposal
that I turned a shoulder
to the church ladies sneering
at market as I handpicked
a bucket of full-bellied oysters
for your supper and chose
the beans for your twice-brewed
coffee, thick as the stench
of guano drifting across the Delaware.

I needed not a man but a sturdy
mantle to hold the remnants
of my former life: my husband's
wool sailing cap, the compass
from his maiden ship, thrown off now
from true direction. You'd have me
think you're a sailor yourself
with your *damns* and *hells*
and orders to *ram a needle*
up the bookbinder's ass.
But I've been close enough
to smell your soap and cologne.
I've filled the bowl by your chair

with mignonette and roses and lilacs,
at your request. And I've seen you
save my lacework shirts
for reading your Mr. Lincoln poem.

We've had our fun:
when *Mr. Trouble*, as I call him,
knocks, I ring the bell three times
as warning. And we laugh
about your room, more full of dust
than Mickle Street after a whorl
comes rolling through. It's safe
to tell you now I only
got a broom in there on days
you took to town in your buggy
pulled by that stiff-kneed pony,
and even then I had to wade
through notes and receipts,
billheads and letters and proofs
and scraps of wallpaper saved
for who knows what. Your life spilled

from that iron-banded double-hasped trunk,
as massive in its own way
as this stone tomb, as the man
you aimed to be.

The Lost Letter

*I took pleasure in taking care of her— she thought everything of
me—when any thing went wrong she would come to me.*
—Lavinia Norcross, aunt of Emily Dickinson

I've failed at my primary employment—
being a person, you said when last you wrote.
Dearest Emily, you've failed only
at not knowing in what you shine. A person
is not simply one who, like your sister,
dusts the stairs and busies herself
with pussies and posies. Young men
may fancy playing spooney with Vinnie,
but with you they wish to talk late into the evening,
after other less spiritual souls have
buried themselves in feather pillows.

Remember the thunderstorm on the way
to Monson, just after we passed Mr. Clapps' place?
You were not quite three, yet you
bellowed *the fire! the fire!*—your first
attempt at poetry. Now you send me such lines as
Oh if remembering were forgetting.
That visit you plucked away at the piano,
calling it *moosic*, the same name you gave
to the songs of the cows at Dillingsworth Dairy.
After you left I found your tiny red apron
by the hearth and used it as a handkerchief
as I wept and wept. You were my child
before my children, and tho I'd never
tell Loo or Fanny, I felt I'd nearly used up
my best love before they came.
Yes, if remembering were forgetting.

Em, dear, I am not well, as I'm sure Vinnie reported
after her visit. She was a perfect nurse,
boiling and scrubbing and fluffing through the week.
But now the simple task of taking air
is the hard work of a fieldhand, and even as I
write this I must pause with my pen
as if summoning great thoughts. No,
that is *your* primary employment. Please
remember not to forget it.

Poe's Last Letter, Abridged

from Edgar Allan Poe's letter to Maria Clemm

Love   is

                        nothing

                        [nothing]

        but   fear

with   a   name

        &   address.

        I   will   marry

                                [marry]

my   own

                [own]

        death.

Calamity Jane at the Dime Museum

It's the showman's place to supply what the public wants, if he can find out what that is.

—George Middleton, who hired Martha Jane Canary Burke (a.k.a. Calamity Jane) as an attraction in his dime museum.

Never trust a man who starts believin'
his own lies, I always say. A woman,

though—that's another story. Miss Jane
could spin a yarn like she was knittin'

sweaters for every sucker who
dreamed of gold. We signed her for

fifty bucks a week and all expenses,
twice what the Fat Lady gets, 'less you

count Big Winny who broke the scales
and the bank. Two shows a day

Miss Jane gave us, and we gave her
top billing—"Scout, Trapper and

Indian Slayer"—which didn't sit too well
with the Aboriginal albino beauty

or Texas Jack, the one-armed whittler.
Even Ralston the Rattlesnake King

was sore, which took some nerve
since his rattlers were tamer than

a litter of purring kittens. But business
is business. And the cost of the costume

was hers to bear: $11 boots and who
knows how much for the buckskins

and the Winchester she cradled like a baby.
It's true she liked a nip . . . or three

or four, *partaking freely of that which
leaveth color on the nose*, as one reporter

wrote. But she weren't no trouble,
really—showed up on time and posed

for photos. We woulda kept her on
for another tour, but there was somethin'

told me she was a one-off act.
The people came and paid their dimes,

shuffled down the hall past fortune tellers
and typewritin' contests to the corner

where Miss Jane sat up on her stool.
What they'd heard about her back

in the day could fill a real museum,
but what they saw was a woman

with hair goin' gray and a mouth
that seems like it'd made up its mind.

She coulda been your teacher in
grade school or the lady sellin' feed

at the general store. You see, folks
have had enough of real life. They want

somethin' curious, somethin' shiny,
somethin' more.

Emma Lazarus's Statue of Liberty Sonnet, Abridged

The   brazen,

         mighty   woman,

     mother   of

                 pomp

with   lips

         yearning   to

      refuse

          our   shore,

send   these   homeless

    to   the

        door.

Mother of Invention

What's a horse in full stride
but alternating currents—
right legs, left legs, right:
a sharing of burdens.

You were only five
the year we lost Dane.
It nearly cost my mind,
but it's you who really paid.

I fear that in our grief,
we left you to the wind,
a freshly-wrung bed sheet
hung without a pin.

Thunder shook the room
the night that you were born.
Thunder shook my womb:
thunder, lightning, moan, moan.

The doctors called it sickness
when your senses went astray.
You could hear the tick tick ticks
of watches three rooms away

and visualize inventions whole
in a sudden mental flood
while I sketched out my tools
on butcher paper flecked with blood.

Thunder shook the room
the night that you unfurled.
Some said you came too soon,
but you were ready for the world.

As a boy, you'd take your bath
out in the sunny yard
and chase after Mačak,
stroking his fur to create sparks.

I can still see your popgun
fashioned from cornstalks,
see you leaping from the barn
with a lady's parasol.

Da-dum-da-dum-da-dum,
like the Marko epics I recall.
In electricity, too, there's rhythm—
in life: *da-dum . . . da . . .*

Thunder shook the room
the night that you arrived.
The midwife said child of storm.
but I saw a child of light.

Facing Manet

> *"M. Manet has exhibited a philosopher trampling on oyster shells,*
> *and a water-colour of his Christ supported by angels. The*
> *[exhibition] Club should try harder."*
>
> —author Edmund Duranty in a Feb. 19, 1870 *Paris-Journal*
> review, which led, four days later, to a fencing duel between
> himself and his friend, Edouard Manet.

Is it true a man's grievances
are heavier than his grief?
You should know, Edouard.
Your salon rejections weigh on you
more, it seems, than the memory
of Alexandre, your *boy with the cherries,*
hanging from the thin cord
in your studio attic, a stick
of barley sugar pressed between
his teeth.

A sculptor I once reviewed
told me this: to sculpt a bird
you start with a block of marble
and take away everything that isn't a bird.
O, if life were marble! I have chipped away
at the space my father should have filled
and found not a man but an angry child
clawing at the clouds. Your own son
limps along with another name
and calls you *godfather.* For shame.
This is not *light dancing on colour,* Eduoard.
This is a carpenter with shattered hands,
a cartographer who has lost his sight.

So, we will fight. We will meet at 11 a.m.
in the Forest of Saint-Germain.
You will wear shoes too generous in size,

bought just for this day. I can already
write the ending: we will collapse
in the grass, laughing, comrades again.
First, you will aim for my chest,
lancing flesh the way you scraped
the palette knife against your Christ's heart.
And you and I, who grip weapons
like a young girl fingers a spider
found creeping in her quarters, will lunge forth,
clumsy and dumb, the way men do in hate
and in love.

Galileo's *Sidereal Messenger*, Abridged

<pre>
        With   this   instrument

                    of   our   senses,

behold   the   moon,

                        naked   and   rough

        as   a   philosopher   wandering

    in   Paris   or   at   sea.

                                                Forsake

caution —   let   ABCD   be

        a   cloud,   a   face,

    a   hand,   the   sun

        as   shadows   lose

    their   blackness

and   become   one.
</pre>

To Nellie, with Love from the Letter E

She was considered the best reporter in America.
—New York Evening Journal's editor Arthur Brisbane on Elizabeth
Cochrane, (a.k.a. Nellie Bly), the first female investigative reporter

For the silent e in Cochrane,
added to your surname to elevate
your status. E for the egging on

of your half-dozen brothers
who dared you to scale the tallest
apple tree and ride the old horse

on your feet. E for the education
on which your judge father insisted,
for the eligible bachelors your mother

paraded, afraid you'd become
a spinster—or worse—a schoolmarm.
E for Erasmus Wilson whose column

"What Girls Are Good For" inspired
your furious retort, for the editor who
hired his first lady reporter for $5 a week,

and for the errand boy who hummed
"Nelly Bly" while cleaning the cuspidor
as the newsroom staff lobbed possible

pennames: *Heigh, Nelly ho, Nelly
listen lub to me,/I'll sing for you,
play for you, a dulcem melody.*

E for your eagerness to read your first
published article that Sunday morning
in Uncle Thomas's parlor as the paper

sat unopened till well after services.
E for your enraged family who feared
this gently-reared cultured girl

would be sent off to the saloons.
E for the exasperation you felt
writing anonymous reviews

of choral society shows—and then,
for your escape to Mexico,
New York and finally, around

the globe in less than eighty days.
E for the experts who declared you
insane, sending you undercover

to Blackwell's Island. E for your exposé
on mental asylums where women were
fed moldy bread and forced to sleep

in rat-infested beds. E for your
searching eyes, grey with flecks of violet.
E for Elizabeth, no longer silent.

Origen de Las Dos Fridas

> *I must have been six years old when I had the intense*
> *experience of an imaginary friendship with a little girl.*
> —Frida Kahlo in her diary, 1950

When your family threw open the balconies
on La Calle de Allende, welcoming
wounded Zapatistas with corn gorditas—

When polio seized you in its grip
like a lover, shriveling your leg
to a whittled stick—

When the streetcar crushed your
spine and spirit, the handrail puncturing
your womb like a matador's sword—

When the doctor locked you inside
an orthopedic corset until you colored
your plaster cage with desire—

When Diego—*tu accidente sugundo*—
set you on fire and watched you burn till you
sought the kind of love he hadn't earned—

When—as a girl—you huffed your pane
of glass and drew a door to our world
where we danced beneath cedron trees—

I was there—hovering like a storm
cloud on canvas—real as your own gaze.

I was your father's vertigo—the strokes
that dulled you mother—your weakness
for a liter of aged tequila—your other.

I was the gold exploding from the artisan's
pouch in the crash—powder sooting
your blood as it seeped the streets.

I was each of the three blank pages
in your diary—and the entries you
yanked like hairs at the root.

I was the country you loved
to love—baroque and broken like
the body you gilded in ribbons and chains.

I was everything you ever wanted
a painting and a man to be:
beautifully brutal, brutally honest.

I was the jangling of your bulbous
jewels announcing your arrival in every
room like an omen—or a promise.

Postcards from Ghost Ranch

1.
Frost clings to windows till noon.
Navajo Canyon lets loose
a gloriously wet sneeze of snow. And later,
bands of white lie in lines, one above the other
like surf coming in, like music.

2.
Your sand hills are clean and hard
and upright like young maidens.
Barrano is full of moonlight tonight,
the sweetness of white pear trees
as stifling as held breath. Onions are sprouting,
bees humming, and the apricots
wear frills of white lace. Time
and cottonwoods can't wait.

3.
First rays of sun in the dandelions.
Peaches straight from the trees, bright
with dew and sweet with August.
Look up at the sky and think of the star
riding along the mesa—the ranch
and the stillness and the stars.
So different from Texas where the air
is soft and grey and you forget the moon,
lock it in a closet. Different even
from Santa Fe, with its weight
of laughter and chatter.

4.

Deer leaping over the mountain,
golden with rain and sunlight.
Piedra Lumbre—the burnt rock—
and the little pink hill you painted,
curling into deep red brown, buttressed
by violet in the evening sun. Above
the western mesa, the evening star
hangs like a plum.

5.

No one can give yourself to yourself,
you told me once, and it's true.
But you gave yourself to me
in teaspoons, bittersweet
as fresh-squeezed lemon juice.

6.

You in a whang doodle of a mood,
climbing the clunky ladder in your plaid skirt
and wide-brimmed hat and plunking
your bony bottom down on the roof,
your smile a dare to anyone
who'd call your bluff.

7.

You on the patio in your metal lounger,
pen poised for your daily letter
to Alfred, your hair yanked back
in a ponytail, the cuffs of your khakis
deep enough to hold everything
I'll never have the pluck to say.

8.
The two of us in the garden,
you in a loose apron, me in a halter,
your hand on my bare shoulder
as I peel the carrots. The midday sun
allows no shadows, no secrets.

9.
Me in my faded Levi's, my hair
tied with a red ribbon, the top
of our mesa stored in my heart.
I believe in this world I see
from my window. I believe in skunks—
pintos: the painted ones—well-larded
with mallards under their ribs.
I believe in the gash of light
dividing summer and fall.
But perhaps this isn't enough.
Perhaps these words say nothing at all.

Assisted Living: Demi-Sonnets

Reverse Alchemy

Forget bullion bricks
and gaudy chains around
the neck. I'm perfecting
the long tradition of turning
gold to lead. See: autumn
leaves. See: lust. See: everyone
you've ever loved who's dead.

Landline

The phone number of my childhood
home. Once I propped our rotary beast
on my lap and asked the operator to connect
me to *my friend Beth*. I said: *She has
red hair and a white cat and she can die
from bee stings.* 288-9041, 288-9041.
If you dial it now, it rings and rings.

Generation Stuck

Cut yourself and you'll get lockjaw,
our mothers warned. *Scowl and your face
will freeze like that.* Every TV rerun
had a quicksand episode: Gilligan
or the kid from *Land of the Lost*
sinking up to his neck. Decades later:
screens, cubicles, debt, regret.

Teeth

Long-neglected picket fence,
ragged chits littering the stockroom
floor, a prized collection of brooches
carved from bones. Open wide
for the mirror. Smile. Find
your weathered name among
the crooked tombstones.

Pulse

The drum that thrums in
blood, a sump pump humming
in a flooded basement, Bedouin
plodding under the plunging sun.
Feel it in your thumb, from
sternum to scrotum. Da-dum,
da-dum, da-dum. Done.

Lung

A raft in a backyard pool,
strand of thread spooled and
unspooled, the sagging bag
in the chemo treatment room,
a cyclist chugging up and coasting
down a hill. We want to inhale
our days. We want our fill.

Good Measure

A baby panda is as big
as a butter stick. A deck
of playing cards equals
one serving of meat.
A bullet's the size of
your pinky tip. We need
oceans to measure our grief.

Safety Drill

In the event of an active shooter,
run in zig-zags behind the school,
my daughter is told. It's harder
to hit a moving target. Run across
the field to the woods. Don't cower.
But: so many moving targets,
so many wind-blown flowers.

The World Reduced to Fists

after Reginald Dwayne Betts

The world reduced to triggers,
to epithets that rhyme with trigger,
to words launched like surface-to-air
missiles. To rumbling stomachs
of hungry kids, to drinking water
the color of piss. The world reduced
to fists. The world reduced to this.

Exonerated

The innocent man is freed
after 19 years in jail. He's afraid
of the TV remote and steel
silverware. He's trained himself
to avoid looking anyone
in the eye. He knows he should
be angry. But oh, the sky.

Worth

You can fall in love with a rich man
just as easily as you can fall in love
with a poor man, our 7th grade teacher
told the class. She spoke as if bequeathing
precious pearls. It took me thirty more
years in the world to learn that her advice
stung the boys as much as it did the girls.

When I Won a Poetry Prize

My daughter, then five, begged me
to buy *a warehouse full of pink light-up*
sneakers in every size so that she'd have
a lifetime supply. Instead, we got vinyl
siding. Her feet are now bigger than mine.
My mind flashes to an image of those
shoes blinking, blinking in the night.

Trick-or-Treat

Halloween night, two black bears
tramped through town. The next day,
we awoke to a blur of fur on the front
page of the local paper. Had we passed
them on the sidewalk, my son a werewolf
under the full moon? Yes, I'm certain
we waved and praised their costumes.

Fall, Central Pennsylvania

Twang of a basketball
on the street, teen dribbling
his way to a pickup game,
the sky a bruised backdrop
for barren trees, cracked
macadam court lacquered
with golden ginkgo tears.

Small Town

My neighbor returns from this week's chemo.
Her friend—a local judge—pedals up
on a 3-speed. She's here to administer
a foot massage. I don't want much. To live
in a town where people ride bikes with baskets,
a place where people show up, take your
beleaguered feet in their hands and rub.

Assisted Living

1. At Sixteen

She ran off to join Major Bowes'
All-Girl Band. First stop: Chicago where
she dropped her father's Italian name,
adopting the "Palmer" from the Hilton
downtown. She headlined with Sinatra
and Pat Boone. And now she shuffles across
the room, naked under a hospital gown.

2. Waiting

The woman who chop-chopped her hands
like cymbals now finds herself waiting
for everything: a sponge bath, a chirpy nurse
to wipe her *bum*, a son to blow in like weather.
Tick tick till lunch, though she can't stand
the food. Tick tick tick till dinner. Tick tick
tick. Here, even the sweet potatoes are bitter.

3. Heart Failure

She's a novel with too many plots,
a photo album with no room for another
shot, an overfilled balloon about to pop.
She's outlived everyone she's loved
or loathed, outlived the very word cause.
She is the last scene in a classic film
frozen on pause.

4. Osteoporosis

The pelvis of a twenty-something woman
is a plumb weight. A nonagenarian's
is as light as Styrofoam. The doctor
warns it could snap with a sneeze.
But your mother is a jet burning off
excess fuel. She wants to hear flute music
blowing through her bones with each breeze.

5. Cure

Doctors have buried the word
cure. We now have treatment
plans and regimens and promises
of new vaccines. We have weeks
or months or years of progression-
free disease. We have years
or months or weeks.

6. Black & White

Pregnant belly under a fox fur coat,
Cape Cod home on a suburban street,
rag-top car in the drive. The new bike
beneath an aluminum Christmas tree,
a son's acceptance to an Ivy League.
This is her world in black & white.
Not pictured: the life she left behind.

7. Daughters of the Depression

Your mother and her cousins wave
from the luau, the pool, the edge
of hotel beds: instamatic proof
of how far they've come, of the men
they didn't take, the meals they didn't
cook, the rooms they didn't clean,
the sweat they didn't break.

8. You Were an Only Child

The only one your dad taught to throw a ball,
ride a bike, shift gears in the blue VW Bug.
Your mother's companion at Broadway shows
and Sunday mass, the reason your folks sat
in the front row for every trombone solo
and line drive. You were an only child. Except
for the first three babies who didn't survive.

9. Tasks for the Living

You attach the walker basket
with the built-in cup holder, the one
that lets her carry a glass of water
to her favorite seat. Before you leave,
you test the battery in her hearing aid,
coax a curl with your finger dabbed
in spit, and kiss her papery cheek.

10. Lean-to

After a morning spent bathing,
buttoning, and hoisting your mother
like an overgrown infant, we find
the one sunlit table in an otherwise
dark sushi place and without speaking,
touch each of our fingertips together:
lean-to, temple, shelter.

11. Let It Be Known

That lake in New Hampshire,
its surface shimmering like
sequins on the gold dress
she wore on tour in 1934,
her body bobbing in pockets
of spring-fed cold. This is how.
This is how she wants to go.

12. Zephyr

You trapped your mother's black cat
in a cage and presented the armful
of squirming fur at her bedside,
vowing to brush him twice a day
and feed him tuna-flavored treats.
That was her cue. The hospice nurse
said our names. And then we knew.

Taxonomies: Demi-Sonnets

Taxonomy of Rasps

Bacall telling Bogie it *depends*
on who's in the saddle. Stevie Nicks
insisting nothing else matters.
Kathleen Turner as Jessica Rabbit.
Patti Smith—because the night
belonged to her. A lusty blur of moan
and scold. They didn't ask. They told.

Taxonomy of Smiles

Ambiguity tugging the seams of Mona Lisa's lips.
Helen of Troy, for surely it wasn't a scowl
that launched a thousand ships. *Smile more*, say men,
always men. But my mouth's default is a grin.
Classic American smile, proclaims my dentist.
What does he mean? Unrestrained? Too much? Larger
than life? When he says *open wider*, I want to bite.

Taxonomy of Canals

Panama, Amsterdam, Venice. Root canals.
Birth canals. The C&D Canal where I biked
with my son tucked into a toddler seat
as oceangoing ships from Russia and China
slid by. Such a brief passage. My son waved
to the men on deck. The men waved back.
They were just passing through. We were, too.

Taxonomy of the Pre-Seatbelt Era

The summer we moved to Appalachia, gray cat
in one box, my baby brother in another. Me riding
shotgun, protected by my mother's arm. My classmate
Sadie who went through a windshield. I pictured
her floating through a slow-motion spray of glass
stars. How did she stitch *Sadie* from *Sarah*? How did
she find herself behind the constellation of scars?

Taxonomy of Taxonomies

From the Greek—*taxis:* order, *nomos:* science.
Rules for an unruly world. When my father
slipped into an unclassified black hole, I saved
babysitting money to paint my bedroom walls
yellow. I studied swatches: Sunny Veranda,
Forsythia, Pollen Powder, Gusto Gold,
each strip a family with the same undertones.

Taxonomy of Dancing

The stand and sway. The full-on
stomping and sweating, every limb
flailing as if it's on fire. The train of hands
on hips, stuttering to a stop when a girl
loses a shoe. My college date who said
You're dancing with the drummer, not me.
The burn in my cheeks because it was true.

Taxonomy of Cell Phones

In 1990 BC—Before Cells—I chatted
with a stranger in a laundromat. We've been
friends ever since. Now a communication device
keeps people from talking to each other, our faces
half-aglow in a screen eclipse. We cradle
phones like baby birds who've slipped
from the nest, feed them from our fingertips.

Taxonomy of Churning

The ocean at night: a vast moonlit loom
weaving blue froth. The Delta Queen's
sternwheel muscling through the Mississippi.
Butter on the prairie, Ma teaching Laura
to plunge the dash in stiffening cream.
Voices boiling over on the TV news, so many
words unleashed from what they mean.

Taxonomy of Field Trips

I learned to pack snacks like an American:
family-sized bags of Doritos, 2-liter bottles
of Coke—apples and water a cardinal sin.
Monticello, Williamsburg, D.C. A perennial fave:
the U.S. Mint where sheets of currency coursed
like blood through veins. We were taught to bow
down at the shrine of green money, white men.

Taxonomy of Shadows

Lean companion strolling beside you
on the beach. Alter ego. Body to the soul.
The man who sold his shadow to the devil.
Shadowless demons. Your twin crow.
The shadow Peter Pan lost and Wendy
reattached. The darkness that pools
around statues celebrating our dark past.

Taxonomy of Endings That Are Actually Beginnings

The last scene of *The Godfather*,
when the closed door shows Michael's
transformation into the boss. Cilantro
that *bolts* mid-summer, leaving behind
coriander seeds. False sunrise teasing
the real thing. The man who knew your mom
was pregnant and left. A knee on the neck.

Taxonomy of Shields

Plastic eyepatch after cataract surgery.
Burglar alarms, pepper spray, air bags.
Antibacterial wipes, vitamins, a seat
in first class. School buses full of bulletproof
backpacks. Foreheads crossed with ash.
How we try to inoculate ourselves against
being shattered in a world made of glass.

Taxonomy of Spills

Milk, but don't cry over it. Black opal
ooze of oil, birds trapped in slick
straightjackets. What's the phrase
for saying too much? Spilled his heart?
No—as if truth is violence—spilled his guts.
Guns kill 100 souls a day. We are all
slipping on sidewalks thick with blood.

Taxonomy of Votes

In some countries, they dip index fingers in ink
to show who voted. Electoral stain. Here, we pull levers
like slot machines. *God gave us sports and weather
so we don't have to talk politics*, a friend complained.
But I don't care about baseball or rain. Remember
the hanging chads, assonant as a garage band name?
Their songs are IEDs that echo in your brain.

Taxonomy of Recipes

Soufflés are tragic. Hollandaise is a breeze.
For a challenge, turn a sweet savory or a savory
sweet. Everything tastes better with chicken broth.
Directions are optional except when they're not.
A macaroon is not a macaron, and neither one
is president of France. Our own sad concoction
of leaders forgot we're a melting pot.

Taxonomy of the Border I

They took the children from their mothers.
They ignored their cries. The children's cries.
The mothers' cries. They took the children
from their mothers. Babies in diapers,
cocooned in woven senkas, girls with pink
butterfly barrettes, boys in red Elmo shirts,
children with sleep in their eyes.

Taxonomy of the Border II

They took the shoes from the children,
gnawed off gummy soles with knives
like whittlers on the porch of a shotgun
house. They slipped laces from the throats
of sneakers and boots, then handed back husks
of canvas and rubber as if to say *Only we have*
the power, the power to make a noose.

Taxonomy of Quarantine

Sanitize touchpoints with Clorox wipes,
stock the pantry with beans & rice. Patch cracked
plaster you see when still. Try not to kill your mate
who chews like a horse galloping on gravel. If masks
fog your glasses, wipe the hazy half-moons hiding
your eyes. Each day is a recipe of equal parts
boredom and fear. Knead a ball of anger. Let it rise.

Taxonomy of Google Autocomplete

What's the Difference—

What's the difference between jelly and jam,
between club soda and seltzer, between
a modem and a router? What's the difference
between llamas and alpacas, mildew and mold,
salamanders and newts? What's the difference
between a passport and visa, brown eggs
and white, stars and planets, me and you?

How Far—

How far can you drive on a spare,
walk in a day, cast a fly rod? How far
can you hear a train's whistle, a lion's roar?
How far can you shoot a gun, hear a shot?
How far can you move after divorce? How far
can you see while crying? How far can you
fall? How far can you fall without dying?

How Many—

How many stripes on a zebra?
How many cups in a quart, feet in
a mile, minutes in a day? How many
years to paint the Sistine Chapel?
How many lives lost in Iraq, children
poisoned in Flint? How many,
how many look the other way?

Taxonomy of Overheard Conversations

Couple at the next table on a blind date,
the high-pitched screech of chair legs on tile
when he stands to leave. Mother and daughter
in a dressing room, the mother saying
You could cover your arm fat with a shawl.
Teenage girl at my gynecologist's office,
her muffled sobs through the thin wall.

Taxonomy of Emptiness

Answer bubbles on a standardized test.
A clean sheet parachuting over
a king-sized bed. Stomachs churning
with hunger or dread. A child's
birthday balloon filled with breath.
How we stitch together the stories
of ourselves with invisible thread.

Taxonomy of Moths

Shale confetti flitting against
a white wall. We tried but failed
to make ourselves small, slipping
sideways through doors to leave
them in the night. Moth: so close
to *mouth*. They're drawn to light
like us. Like us, they turn to dust.

Taxonomy of Mouths

Origin of longing, home
for nourishment and song.
How we first connect, lip
and spit and tongue—later,
how we split apart, each word
a volley. Where the river
empties itself into another body.

Taxonomy of Physical Markings

Dimples, those adorable genetic defects.
Grandmother puckering a newborn's
toes to check for lucky stars on his feet.
Some people wait their whole lives
to learn from lovers that they're harboring
birthmarks on intimate parts. Some never
find out what it's like to be seen.

Taxonomy of Knots

My talent for untangling necklaces.
That half-finished scarf, its umbilical
cord of snarled yarn. The newly
discovered twisted squid contorting
in the darkest depths of the Gulf.
My son's varsity soccer teammate
who hanged himself in the barn.

Taxonomy of Things I Miss

Movie theatres with sound
from a single source. The coziness
of telephone booths. Toll collectors
who know the route. Mood rings.
Kids running through sprinklers
on front lawns. The crackle
of a turntable needle between songs.

Taxonomy of *Mid-*

Midsize: the Goldilocks of cars.
Midday: light shows all your scars.
Mid-sentence: when you try—
Mid-semester, mid-winter, mid-thigh.
Mid-century, midnight, midwife.
When every memory is a pang
prying open your heart: midlife.

Taxonomy of Menopause

Estrogen, like Queen Esther from the Bible
if she had spared her people then perished.
You are hollowed out like a cored apple,
a pill bottle with a single tablet rattling inside.
Hole that can't be patched, itch that
scratches back. Everything is burning.
You are on fire and lighting the match.

Taxonomy of Turbulence

Passengers and bags jounce like balls
in a lottery machine. You win if you
walk away cussing but not concussed.
The pilot did not warn us about rough air
or layoffs or divorce or white islands
on an X-ray. He says *Welcome to Boston*
when we thought we'd landed in LA.

Taxonomy of Mirages

The way desert light bends
to become water: a magic spell.
Trickster mirrors reflecting older
selves. How we're the same bodies
even as we shed and renew our cells.
What I was writing when I thought
I was writing something else.

Taxonomy of Fairy Tales

Humpty Dumpty chants
Build that wall. The piper
lures all the rats to town.
The huntsman targets
everyone who isn't white
as snow. The wolf huffs & puffs
& blows the world down.

Fluent in Blue

I-95 Corridor

1.
This is where I was cited
for reckless driving
and my uncle quipped
95 is the route number,
not the speed limit.

2.
This is where I stopped
with an ex-boyfriend
on the last stretch from Miami
and a motel clerk asked
if we wanted the *all night*
or *hourly* rate.

3.
This is where my grad school
U-Haul broke down and I
waited for the wrecker
with a Swiss Army knife
flexed against my bare thigh.

4.
This is where I learned
all the lyrics to Dylan's
"Subterranean Homesick Blues,"
rewinding the cassette
till it snapped in the deck.

5.
This is where I interviewed
for an adjunct teaching gig
that would cost me more
in tolls and gas than I'd earn.

6.
This is where thieves
took my Plymouth Breeze
for a joyride then dumped it
on the shoulder, my just-cashed
paycheck still in the console.

7.
This is where my husband
missed an exit for the symphony
and grazed a concrete pillar
beneath an underpass.

8.
This is where I ordered
my daughter vanilla ice cream
with extra maraschino cherries
after she lay corpse-still
for her first echocardiogram.

9.
This is where a tanker truck
caught fire, melting the highway's
steel beams until an entire span
collapsed like a ruptured aorta.

10.
Corridor:
a long,
narrow
passage
between
rooms
or land.
Or time.

11.
They are still sifting through
the truck driver's remains.

12.
I can never remember
if it's *steel oneself*
or *steal oneself*. Am I
supposed to harden my feelings
or shove them under
my shirt like a shoplifter?

13.
In the show I'm watching,
one corridor leads
to another, rough cut
after rough cut of white walls
in a workplace maze.

14.
The day of the symphony,
we abandoned our SUV
on the off-ramp and ran
four blocks to the concert hall,
plunking into plush seats
just in time for *da da da dum*.

15.
Commute, hospital, concert,
wedding, commute, bar mitzvah,
commute, funeral, commute.

16.
Lately I need to sit
closer to the throat
of a bass trombone
or purring cat to feel
a stirring in my pulse.

17.
My uncle is gone now,
a stroke two days
before Christmas.

18.
For years I replayed
that last conversation
in my ex's red Jetta,
his hands trying to bend
the steering wheel,
his eyes swollen.

19.
What's the difference
between carefree
and careless?

20.
I'm not sure
I want to know.

21.
So many bodies
and bodies in motion.

22.
I can't steal myself.
I'm already stolen.

To the Man Who Stole Our Pregnant Dog

I hope she bit you, shredding the flesh
of the hand that wooed her from my childhood

yard. You probably sold her pups off the back
of a rusty truck at a flea market, a handwritten

sign missing an *s* or a *t* in *Bassett Hound*.
What I remember: her banana peel ears

swept the ground like unhemmed drapes.
We called her Blarney, and I'd already

named the babies after other Irish castles
from the set of pleather-bound Britannicas

we bought by the month. Every evening
for weeks, I sat in the bath after the water turned

cold, thinking my discomfort would bring her
home. The walls shuddered with the last

rumblings of my parents' marriage. I slid
under to see how long I could go without air,

the soapy surface a scrim over a body
that was there, then not there.

Among the Beasts

We packed picnics—Ritz crackers and grapes,
bottles of Coke—and sat among the dead:

a beloved beagle who was now *chasing balls*
in heaven, a 20-year-old calico *gone too soon.*

Graves were marked with lacquered photographs
and poems, cracked and yellow from the sun.

Someone had buried a horse. Its tombstone
was a life-sized thoroughbred reigning over

the smaller beasts. This was pre-Stephen King,
pre-zoning that would prohibit a pet cemetery

in the center of a subdivision. Once we saw
a funeral for a German shepherd. The owner—

a teary middle-aged man—peeled back
a black garbage bag to reveal a stiff head,

an open jaw. I thought of the science experiment
from class: our teacher dipped a goldfish

in liquid nitrogen, then shattered it on his desk,
bits of orange scattering like glass. The boys

laughed. In that brief moment of shock, I darted
to collect the shards and reassemble them

like a puzzle or a memory. Then the teacher asked
for a volunteer to scoop the pieces into the trash.

Impala

for Stephanie

Kickball on my dead-end street,
you bowling the red rubber ball,
me launching it toward that recurring
suburban sky. Then creeping by:

the beige sedan, hovering and purring
like the *Close Encounters* mother ship.
Impala. And all I could think was *pale*,
pale as the ass of the man who flashed

us, then fled, slipping our stunned faces
into his pocket like a snapshot, leaving us
with a lifetime of taking license plates
whether we needed to or not.

Flood

I grew up in the capital
of the Confederacy,

my skin darkened
only by the shadows

of Monument Avenue.
Once the James River

flooded and the two whitest
boys from my high school

ignored warnings
and tooled around

in a canoe until the waters
took them. For days

their buttoned-down
faces were on the news

as helicopters swooped
and searched. They were

found clinging to a tree,
muddy and cold but unhurt.

More than a house
with a pool in the suburbs.

More than tuition
at a brick college

with a cupola. More than
a guided hunting trip

to Alaska where you sleep
in a luxury yurt. That's

how much the rescue cost.
They did not think:

*moonlit bank where
my ancestors were*

*dragged from ships
or branch from which*

bodies once swung.
They did not have to.

They did not have to
question their worth.

Sibilant

From the Latin, *sibilans*: hissing or whistling,
as in *She sells sea shells, Sing a song of sixpence.*

Smiles and *silence* and *pleasure* and *sorrow.*
How the same tongue that shushes you to sleep

can slide so easily into a snake's vicious whisper
tomorrow. My father taught me shot put, brought chocolate

to my seventh-grade track meet for a burst of speed.
My father shut himself behind doors for days,

emerging only to eat. Some linguists insist
th, *f*, *z*, and *v* sounds are not truly sibilant,

merely half-siblings of *s*, like the daughter
my father conceived with his second wife, their marriage

a brief flutter, a flashpoint before his darkness
settled in like river mist. *Mist. Missed.*

Things I've assumed my younger brother and half-sister knew:
That his '68 Mustang was dark green, not black.

That once when it stalled on an overpass
in a freak Virginia blizzard, we slung groceries

over our shoulders and slid six blocks
to our father's basement apartment, his first since

the divorce. That the bathroom had tiles the color
of Pepto Bismol. That our father was a chemistry equation

and the ghost of chalk after the lesson is erased.
That he loved us. That he loved us all.

That First Summer

Most weekends we packed our blue canoe
with a tent, sleeping bags, books, a cooler,
and enough food and wine for the weekend,

then paddled out to a sand bar in the middle
of the river. For two days we swam and read
and drank and fucked, stretching out in the sun,

lean and dark. Later we learned that some nights
engineers release waters from the dam upstream
to control the floodplain. Experienced boaters

knew to check the schedule. What did we know?
Nothing about harnessing nature, everything
about being swept away.

Dear Son

Do you remember the birthday cake
in the back of the black cab? The frosting

was turquoise, bright as waves of silk
unspooled by street vendors we sped past

in North Wembley. We were late
to a Manchester United game,

the tickets your surprise gift. I flicked
the lighter but could not summon a spark.

Our driver mumbled something in Urdu,
then double-parked alongside a corner store.

Moments later he returned, cupping
in his hands a single lit match. Breath held

and steps measured, he made his way
across an invisible balance beam. A decade

earlier, I had done the same. I kissed
each of your ten candles with the flame.

Vaughn

A boy, a boy with pimples and a coltish gait,
has died. A boy, the younger brother
of my daughter's friend, has died, has taken

his own life. I watched him play in the pool,
hour after hour of splat ball and Marco Polo,
summer after summer, as he grew taller

than his sister. Still, she'd spread his towel
to dry in the sun and wait for him at the end
of the day as he stabbed his wet feet

into flip flops. White mother, Black father
in a part of Pennsylvania where pickups
wave Confederate flags under a bruised

sky. All four of them—parents and kids—
have *V* names. Such hope in those names,
their own little club of safety and love.

Once Vanessa stayed at our house
for a birthday sleepover. The next morning
the girls were going to Galactic Ice,

an indoor rink that blasts pop music.
As she buttoned her coat, her $5 bill
floated to the floor and our dog ate it,

swallowed it whole. Everyone laughed
except Vanessa who cried hard, as if
she saw the entire day playing out—

her friends skate-dancing backwards
and eating French fries in the snack bar—
while she sat home alone. I scrambled

for my wallet and handed her a ten.
Her sobs turned to deep breaths. Then: calm.
How simple it was to ease her pain then.

The Week My Son Leaves Home

At the red light
I can see inside

the fast-food place
with the atrium

playground. A mother
wipes the face

of a child who tries
to pry himself away

from her, eager to return
to the cylinder slide.

      Surely there is a physics model for this—

the tug and the pull.
I can feel his warm

gummy hands
in mine, sticky

with juice. I can
feel him slip loose.

18-Year-Old Daughter as Runaway Horse

Her father searches the streets and alleys,
imploring passersby with photos on his phone—
those dark eyes, the glossy black coat.

I stay behind, opening and closing the stall,
recreating sounds I hope will draw her home: tongue
click of the latch. The hinge—that low moan.

Poem for My Children's Friends

This poem is for Caleb whose mother died
from an overdose the morning he was supposed

to take the SATs, who joined the Air Force
and spent three years in South Korea

and another two in Idaho where he learned
from YouTube videos how to make

dining room tables that he sold weekends
at farmer's markets in Boise.

This is for Huck Finn lookalike Cody
who'd never been outside of our small town

until we took him to Baltimore to see
The Lion King at the Hippodrome. His head

was so filled with stories of urban violence
that he thought the prongs on a bike rack

were two machine guns mounted on the back
of a Honda Civic. This poem is for Vanessa

whose baby brother shot himself in the head.
Vanessa, who stepped forward

from the commencement chorus for a solo,
all the pain and pieces of her shattered

family filling the stadium's empty spaces.
This is for Emily who got engaged

to a guy a month after she met him online.
This is for Mark whose family dresses up

in suits and flowered dresses each Sunday
morning, then sits in the living room to watch

church services on TV. Connor, who works
for Amazon and lives in a Manhattan apartment

with a rooftop pool does not need this poem.
Not yet. But I

will leave an opening for him the way I stocked
the basement mini-fridge with Gatorade

and snacks for kids who crowded the futon
to play video games, explosions and groans

and cheers wafting upstairs. Once my son
butt-dialed me from a friend's house

when a group of boys were talking
about religion. *What if*, my son asked,

all of the stories in the Bible
are like Greek myths—you know, made up

to explain stuff we don't understand?
I listened hard for his friends' responses

but could hear only their muffled objections.
This poem is for the friend born Laura

who transitioned during sophomore year,
who spent weeks searching

lists of boy names, trying them on like
polo shirts and khaki pants. And this is for

the AP history teacher who crossed out
Laura in her gradebook and wrote *Lance*.

When One Has Lived a Long Time in a Small Town

You see the good oral surgeon
    walking down 11th Avenue,
        the one who removed the tooth
            the bad oral surgeon screwed up.

        You still have the x-ray: the drill bit
      embedded in the root of your molar,
  a perfect corkscrew for the world's
tiniest bottle of wine. In a tavern,

you order a drink from a waiter
    who—in eighth grade gym class—
      called your son a *f*g*. As he
        delivers a flute of Prosecco

      to your booth, you feel
    a pang for the boy, now man,
  who no doubt was figuring out
if this town was big enough

for his own desires.
    At the symphony you sit
      next to the owner of a charter company
        who, back in the 70s, took fifteen buses

      to see Kiss perform in Pittsburgh.
    On the way home, it snowed,
  stranding the fleet and all
800 passengers on Route 22.

Tonight's guest performer
	is the son of a woman
		you used to know. Back then,
			he was a pre-teen who loved piano,

			and now, doctorate in hand, he's back
		in Altoona to play "Rhapsody in Blue"
	with the local orchestra, pounding
his way to a sweat so glossy

he'll toss his slippery eyeglasses
	onto the concert grand. The march
		at minute five sounds like freight trains
			thundering through our town, the echo

		of a booming railroad empire
	bouncing off brick buildings.
	In a museum across the tracks,
there's a 1924 photo of Babe Ruth

who crushed the ball
	from Cricket Field to Lexington
		and 7th Street. Today, he would have
			hit a convenience store called Sheetz.

		When one has lived a long time
	in a small town. By *one* I mean
	you, and by *you* I mean *I.*
Once in a city far from here,

I heard Galway Kinnell read from
	his book *When One Has Lived*
		a Long Time Alone, and the reading
			was so long that I thought, ungenerously,

No wonder you live alone, man.
And now I'm guilty of writing
long poems no one will want to hear.
I guess what I'm trying to say

is that I'm growing uncertain
with certainty. I am certainly
uncertain. The good oral surgeon's
daughter brought home a mini pig.

It turns out there's no such thing
as a mini pig. It grew to 300 pounds.
Some pig. If that's not a metaphor for life
in a small town, I don't know what is.

My late mother-in-law, who lived
99 years, was a concert pianist.
When she entertained fellow residents
in the senior home down the block, she closed

each show with "Rhapsody in Blue."
On her 100th birthday, I woke
to the sound of a piano at 5 a.m.
and shook my husband.

He recognized her signature
flourishes and trills and tiptoed
downstairs during the bursting
blue-note riff of the finale.

But there was no one at the piano,
just the blue-dark shadows of dawn.
Later we'd deduce that the cat had
stepped on the CD player remote

that just happened to cue
        the recording she'd made
            at a local studio, the owner
                of which is running the sound board

                at tonight's symphony. He says
            he'll text me when his jazz band
        is playing next month at Spring Dam.
Sometimes when I tell the story

of our mystery pianist, I embellish
        and say my husband grabbed a bat,
            building suspense with words the way
                Gershwin built tension with notes.

            My only ghost story, I like to say.
        But when one has lived a long time
    in a small town, maybe everything's
a ghost story. Maybe we're all ghosts.

Sentence

An oncoming car just misses a squirrel
which darts to a patch of grass,
picks up a black nut and begins nibbling
as if nothing has happened. My daughter asks
*Do you think squirrels get that feeling
like 'I almost died?'*

Thirteen months ago, my daughter
was stopped at a red light at 9:41 p.m.
when a drunk driver of a two-ton pickup
plowed into her from behind. Her car
was totaled. Her body was less damaged—
soft tissue injuries, doctors called them.
The cops said she was lucky to be alive.
The driver was handcuffed and installed
in the back of a squad car, and we returned
to our routines: school, work. She went
to physical therapy a few times a week.
There was a plea agreement, but when
the man showed up drunk to the hearing,
they sent him to prison.

I've heard that squirrels don't remember
where they buried their nuts. Chances are
when they find one, it was planted
by a fellow rodent. Sometimes when
I see a squirrel dig up an acorn in my yard,
I imagine him patting himself
on his little squirrel back and saying,
*What a good idea it was for me to hide
this nut right here where I'd find it!*

How easy it is to anthropomorphize
animals. How difficult to humanize some

humans. The man who hit my daughter
is a welder. I pass his shop every day
on my way to work. It seems he does
mostly routine jobs—machine parts, pipes—
but out front there are a few art pieces
on display: an eagle in flight, a tree with
cursive limbs. A scrolled arch says *For rent—
perfect for weddings*. The month he was
incarcerated, there was a handwritten note
on the door. I never got close enough to read it.

When my daughter asked about the squirrels,
I didn't think about her accident. Most days
I give the man only the smallest thought,
like my late grandmother crossing herself
as she passed a church. Other days I drive by
and it hits me—literally hits me, like I've been
slammed in the gut by an invisible battering ram.
All the air is sucked from my lungs and it's—
I—can't—I—try—she—almost—I—

Son Mother Blues

They may as well be girls when they're young
Smooth skin, loose curls, moon eyes when they're young
Want to sleep wedged up beside you when they're young
Braid your hair, paint your nails, confide when they're young
Bellies full of questions, hungry minds when they're young
Till they learn to hide, bide their time, bite their tongues

Send a boy into the world and hope he makes it home
Send a dark boy into the dark world and hope he makes it home
Angry men waiting at every turn
Angry men with guns waiting at every turn
Angry men with guns and badges waiting at every turn
They beat you
Beat you down
Beat you down till you turn

They make you say yes
Make you say yes
Yes, sir
Yes, sir
Yes, sir
Make you say yes
Till you burn
Till we burn

Dear Rita

*In July 1971, Rita Curran, 24, was found strangled in her
apartment in Burlington, Vermont. More than fifty years later,
authorities used DNA from a cigarette butt to identify her killer:
her upstairs neighbor.*

You were born the same year as my mother
and like my mother became a *schoolteacher*,

the language from today's news frozen in the 70s
like you. One of three careers open to girls—

yes, *girls*—back then: teacher, secretary, nurse.
Or, for the lucky ones, *stewardess* with its fantasy of soaring

far from the New England factory town where summers
were spent screwing caps onto toothpaste tubes

for a fraction of minimum wage. Your killer
was cooling off after a fight with his wife

and likely took his rage out on you. Maybe your red hair
reminded him of her. Or maybe any woman would do,

any body he could break. And then what, a smoke
in your room before trudging upstairs to crawl

in bed beside his alibi? He died decades ago, taking
these answers to his grave. In the photo, you wear

a black choker. Choker: *a necklace or ornamental band
of fabric that fits closely around the neck*. Choker:

one who chokes. If you had lived, you'd be retired
like my mother who texts me pictures of hummingbirds

at her feeder. Always the teacher, she explains
that the male's ruby throat—*gorget*—is named

for a knight's breastplate. The pale wings of females
blur against the gray sky as if they've been erased.

Hide-and-Seek

Northern Virginia, 2002

The week I teach poetry to fourth graders,
my students scramble up slides at recess

and blister their fingers on monkey bars.
They swipe the shoulders of each other's

striped t-shirts and erupt in a chorus
of *Not it! Not it!* They are not squirming

in desks, locked down because a sniper
is targeting strangers. A teen in search

of a father is not crouching in the trunk
of a blue Chevy Caprice, taking aim

at bus passengers and landscapers
and drivers pumping gas. On this day,

a 25-year-old woman vacuums Cheerios
from the back seat of her mini-van

at a Shell station and returns home
to her toddler daughter whose favorite

word is why. *Why dogs bark? Why
thunder go boom? Why babies cry? Why?*

Why? A liquor store clerk rings up
the last sale of the night and heads back

to his garden apartment where he falls
asleep to *Law & Order* re-runs.

Their families will not have to ask *why*. I write
personification on the board. *What word*

is hiding inside? I ask. I'm looking, of course,
for person. In this version, there is only one boy

in the world hungry for attention, and he shoots
his arm in the air and answers *cat*.

Yearlings

Our motion detecting camera captures
a yearling deer at 2:06 a.m. In the grainy
black and white clip, he takes tentative steps

on our square of lawn: a circus performer
on stilts, wobbly piñata. Ears like two blades
of a ceiling fan, rear legs splayed,

knobby as the spindles of an upright Steinway.
I read once that Victorians draped piano legs
because they looked too human,

too titillating. [*Look it up*, I would tell
a student writing this poem.] What was I
dreaming about at that moment? Most likely

the upcoming election, how the president
turned all our televisions black. We reached
into our empty screens to retrieve armfuls

of darkness. In class this week we read a poem
in which the speaker compared school busses
to goldfish in a stream. *What came first,*

a young woman asked, *the busses or the fish?*
This semester my students are a Brady Bunch
grid of faces, our class remote due to the pandemic.

They are taking their first steps into poetry.
You've gotta crawl before you can walk,
people say. But my own children

never crawled. They sat like small Buddhas
till they were almost fourteen months old,
then went straight to toddling.

It's late October. Every day I see bodies
of deer smeared across roadways—
bloody and disemboweled, entrails rutted

by tire tracks. Sometimes one seems
to be sleeping on the shoulder, no visible sign
of injury—clipped, no doubt, internal bleeding.

[Here's where I'd say read William Stafford:
I thought hard for us all—my only swerving—,
then pushed her over the edge into the river.]

545 migrant children may never
see their parents again. *Unreachable,*
our government deems them.

The yearling sniffs the sideview mirror
of my car, then startles, as if
his name has just been called.

He leaves a brushstroke in his wake
like breath against cold night air.
I think hard for us all.

The World is a Scented Handkerchief

after Shakir Li'aibi

The world is a moonlit rib,
      a disheveled vigil, a shackled

clock. The world is greedy
      geography, empty bells,

unripened tides, breathless
      shells on a desert beach.

The world is a newborn
      nun. The world is a fluttering

gun. The world is extinguished
      chants, listless ships, bleeding

thieves. It is clouded vowels,
      the taste of sound on the tongue

of a young girl. The world
      is every word unfurled.

Once you've seen a bird in your house,

you can never not see a bird in your house.
Every rustling paper, every curtain twisting

in a breeze, every shadow on a ceiling
is a frantic, fluttering bird. One winter we had

three in three weeks. I came home to find
our typically docile calico in the kitchen

feasting on a dead robin, her teeth bared,
face pasted with feathers. The house was sealed,

no obvious holes in the siding, windows,
or chimney, not like those buildings ripped open

by storms—giant dollhouses dripping
with insulation, beds and tables still in place,

paintings teetering over sofas. Don't get me
wrong—I'd never welcome destruction.

But I like to glimpse the cross-section
of others' lives. Through the rowhouse wall

we share with neighbors, we don't hear
voices, but sometimes there's a low rumbling

that would barely register a 1.0 on the conversation
Richter scale. Most mornings we hear their shower

pulsing behind our bed. Less than a foot away
a naked man is working his hair into a lather—

just once, I'm sure, because no one
believes those shampoo instructions telling us

to rinse and repeat, do they? When I was a child
we always rented one Days Inn motel room

for our family of four, and my parents hung a sheet
between their bed and ours, a makeshift partition.

I think this is true and not something I saw on TV.
Or maybe I just want to believe they liked each other

once. There are a million years between *is* and *was*,
are and *were*. It's no accident that houses have stories.

Ours has a foundation made of blocks. Sometimes
light squeezes through the cracks. Sometimes a bird.

Porpoises

Slick as oil, they stitch
the waves, scalloped

edge of a black doily.
On the horizon

of the heart monitor,
my father's rhythm

lifts and dips.
ICU. *I see you.*

But I haven't seen him
in years. The doctors

will—what? *remove?*
unplug? disconnect?

him from life support.
What came first,

the brain bleed or the fall?
How many days

was he unconscious
on the floor? How many

decades was he disconnected
from the world?

Father and daughter,
the *r* a liquid consonant

absorbed by air, such a small
role in each word.

As the oldest, I am executor.
I am executioner.

Porpoise, like purpose:
The *why*. I follow the blip

of fins in the distance
until they grow faint,

then disappear. The sea
flatlines beneath the sky.

After/Before

An artist friend has traded
detailed scenes of farms

and streams for small fields
of color during quarantine.

Rothko Postcards, he calls
these gestures of sky and wheat.

My late mother-in-law
once confessed to me

she'd had a near affair
when my husband was young.

The man, also married,
was superintendent of schools.

We were this close, she said,
squeezing between her fingers

an invisible precious stone.
She sat with him in the front seat

of her blue Buick in the board of ed
parking lot to say she was choosing

her current life—
then drove home to dress

the dinner salad with oil and vinegar
the way I'd see her do decades later,

quick flicks of her wrists
like brushstrokes in the kitchen air.

Square of green, square of blue.
Square of orange, square of red.

Representational, abstract. Sunrise.
Sunset. Hard dash of the horizon—

below/above, after/before—
the independent clause of regret.

Anthimeria

using one part of speech as another

My sea gown scarf'd about me,
Hamlet said, verbing his attire.

My daughter likes her likes
on the socials and hearts pics

on the 'Gram. We front and friend,
rebrand brands, and rarely shop

local. Adults keep adulting,
sandwiched between parents

and kids. We don't read books—
we book flights or tourist trips

to the moon and Titanic's grave.
If submersible were only an adjective,

we wouldn't have lost five souls
in an underwater mini-van.

Man is used to being trapped in
cars, buildings, mines, caves.

Are we there yet? Are we? Are we?
You keep samin' when you oughta be

changin' goes the Nancy Sinatra song.
Every part of speech is a noun.

I want to person/place/thing you
from the cold, the blue, the gone.

Azul

Dupont Circle

Before we huddle under a café heater
in early spring sun and sample several

of the seventy tequilas, before we take a selfie
to send our grown kids in other cities

(*No, higher so you can't see our double chins!*),
before we walk thirty-two blocks—

a block for every year we've been together—
stopping just once to beg for the bathroom code

at Starbucks, before we notice the first nodule
of a cherry blossom peeking out

like a tiny pink tongue, before we make love
and doze on the starched hotel sheets,

before all of this, we're at the Phillips
for the Picasso show, his *Período Azul,*

where, next to "Two Women at a Bar,"
hangs a black and white photograph of his studio

from 1902 in which an early incarnation
of the painting rests upside-down on an easel

beside a pinned image of Rodin's "The Thinker,"
the musculature of the sculpture rhyming

with the women's sinewy shoulders and spines,
not unlike a poet pairing *musculature* and *sculpture,*

not unlike the elderly couple shuffling behind us
in the gallery, hunching before each blue scene,

their navy blazer and sweater bleeding
into a single garment, the *tick tick tick*

of her cane on the floor, the insistent whisper
of his portable oxygen machine.

The Internet of Things

(n.): the networking capability that allows information to be sent and received by objects and devices

The low tide riverbed silt
    of things. The cloud-swept

distant hill of things.
    The open bedroom window

in spring of things.
    The moonlit cricket

symphony of things.
    The pitter-patter

tin roof rain of things.
    The fifty-year marriage

loose skin of things.
    The clipped winter light

of things. The stippled lymph
    node of things. The grief.

Oh—the grief. The brief
    ecstatic flight of things.

Human Resources

Indigo

I'm training the new girl just in
from down river. She comes clutching
a flour sack her momma stuffed

with all her worldlies: a whittled spoon
and a rag baby made of cotton scraps,
the smile drawn on with a pencil.

When she asks how to call me, I say Indigo,
though it's not my given name, to tell
the truth. Indigo like the flower we grow

in the fields. Indigo 'cause the Master's boy
looked at me one day and said to Missus,
"Mama, her skin's so black it's blue."

Sophie, Louisa, Josephine, Polly, Rosille, Philis, Lucie.

Her name is Cecilia, says call her Cilly.
She's to help me with the cooking
in the kitchen out back. I show her

how to hang a pig from hooks
in the rafters, how to chop little wheels
of okra on the block, how to keep the fire

going under the pots. Six meals a day
for 300 souls, three a day for the house,
another three for the rest of us.

Feliciana, Magdalaine, Clara, Angelica, Pauline, Esnée, Celeste.

July hits you like a big old wall of heat
and the cook fires make it hotter still,
like taking a bath in a sugar kettle.

Cilly about near faints her first day,
so I teach her my trick: tie a wet cloth
'round your neck.

Isabelle, Marinette, Rose, Florestan, Philomene, Felicite, Claire.

The Missus has one job: to make
sure we do ours. She watches us
from the doorjamb, wiping

her soft hands down the side of her skirts
like they need cleaning. Always fix
the trays of food in the side pantry

before serving, I explain to Cilly.
The staging area, Missus calls it.
Nobody wants to see how it got done.

Etienne, Hortense, Honoré, Fanny, Dosse, Cloé, Adelaide.

I teach her how to keep the cold goods cold
in the olive jar and how to snip sugar.
Missus takes one snip—Master, he likes two.

I show her how to pour the wine
and rum and then stand aside
till they motion for more. Your feet get

weary-tired on the brick floor, but we can't
have rugs on account of the flooding.
The Mississippi gives no warning

before it pays a visit—we've got to haul
the table and chairs upstairs
when waters start licking at the doors.

Clementine, Delphine, Betsie, Marianne, Noel, Caroline, Zepherine.

Cooking beats churning the sugar,
I tell Cilly—that's round-the-clock work.
Barattez, barattez, barattez!

Nights you see candles winking
and hear the paddles scraping against
copper kettles, the wind whipping
palm fronds, men groaning when sugar
leaps up like foam from a mad dog,
burning them on the arms and face.

Ebram, Jacob, Andre, Bellick, Thomas, Lucien, Norbert.

I catch Cilly staring at the parlor ceiling
painted fancy by that artist from Italy.
He took sick and the Missus let him stay,

so he repaid her with more pictures.
The man, he talked funny, but the Missus,
she giggled at every word that came

out of his mouth. "Those pictures
aren't for your eyes," I tell Cilly.
"Your eyes belong on the ground."

I say, "You look up and they'll think
you're trying to be like God above—
or worse, like them."

Elvina, Virginia, Eliza, Nelly, Charlotte, Jenny, Rosella.

One of these days I'll tell her about Sarah,
the girl with teeth so white and pretty,
like a string a shimmery pearls. The Missus

caught her smiling wide in a china plate
admiring all those shiny teeth smiling back.
The Missus won't have that.

Next thing we know the caretaker
drags Sarah down to the blacksmith shop,
lays her head on the anvil,

and knocks her perfect pearls out
one by one. Poor girl's got a mouthful
of darkness now.

Marie, Patrice, Coralie, Dorothy, Lise, Rose, Erasie.

I show her how to warm the sheets
with a coal pan, how to slide it under
the covers real slow. Don't warm Master's bed

with your own self, I warn, but I can't tell
if she hears me right. She's young
but not too young—this much I know.

A man named Living. A woman named Time.
A girl named Girl. A boy named Son.
And me, Indigo. Indigo trade. Indigo dye.

Nobody wants to see how it got done.

Rana Plaza

Savar, Bangladesh

My father was in hospital
that day, his pulse as low as

the Bangshi during dry season.
I wanted to stay with him,

but we were warned *No time off*
for illness, not even your own.

Had he died—which, *Alhamdulillah,*
he did not—the bosses would

have said, *Nothing to be done.*
If he's dead, he's dead.

And so I left my father's side.
It was 8:10 a.m. when I arrived.

Workers gathered by the gate,
afraid. Reshma squeezed

my arm. In my mind there is
a photograph of her wearing that

purple and red salwar kameez.
Inspectors were here, she breathed

into my ear. *They say it is unsafe.*
We had all seen the cracks. Up close,

the building sounded like someone
chewing uncooked rice. And who

was surprised? Each day crews
added more floors, it seemed,

like a tower of toy blocks waiting
to topple. I am not the type

to complain. I am grateful
for work. One who cannot

read or write cannot expect
the privileges of the rich. I sew

until midnight most shifts. I sew
to feed my boys and send them

to school where I hope they learn
what they need to make

a better life. Reshma and I
hesitated. The bosses said

Don't worry, mahilaa, it's fine
and herded us through the door

like goats. *Come, come*, they said,
We have orders to fill. I turned

on my machine, a workhorse:
100 stitches per second,

so smooth it's like sewing
through ghee. If I could

afford one of my own, I would
take in jobs in our home.

It would be cramped, with all
of us in one room, but I could

roll the boys' beds during the day.
That morning, as I sat down

on my stool, I felt a shudder
and then, in a flash, the walls

were gone and the floor fell
away from my feet. I was buried

to my hips in a pile of concrete.
It took nine hours for help to come

and many more to pull me free.
But no Reshma, no Reshma,

whose name means *like silk*.
They found her two and a half

weeks later. She had survived
on rainwater and biscuits

scavenged from the rucksacks
of the dead. Even now she carries

their dust in her mouth.
Others were not as lucky.

Grandmothers, women with young
children, girls not old enough

to marry. Sweet Mita who
always bit her bottom lip

as she fed rivers of fabric
across the plate. So many lost

their lives that day. But if we
had refused to go upstairs,

we would have lost our jobs.
So we obeyed.

The Boys from Atalissa

*Beginning in the 1960s, dozens of men with intellectual disabilities
spent more than thirty years working at a turkey plant in Atalissa,
Iowa, in exchange for room and board and the false promise of
retirement on a ranch in Texas.*

1. Willie Levi

Hang 'em doggone turkeys, boy,
they says to me. *Hang 'em good!*
And so I grabbed 'em by the legs

and yanked 'em out the coop.
Them birds was 40 pounds apiece,
'bout as much as I weighed

when I was brung on as a boy.
Talkin' turkey, that was my thing.
I'd gather up a solid wad of spit

in the back of my mouth and make
a sound like I was garglin'
salt water and bein' strangled

at the same time. And the birds
gurgled right back at me like we was
havin' a regular conversation.

I'd pat 'em on the belly and say
Okay, Tom, quiet on down now,
quiet on down, Tom, and then

when they quit their fidgetin',
I shoved 'em in the shackles
and sent 'em down to the kill room.

After that, the other boys
reached in for the livers and guts
and cut out the hearts.

'Bout 18,000 birds a day, more
'round Thanksgiving time. We was
covered in blood and when you

couldn't see no more, you stopped
to wipe your face, then did it all over
again. They say we make stuff up.

They say one of us gets to fibbin'
and the rest of us chime in like
we're repeatin' prayers at church.

But I ain't a liar. They didn't treat
us like they should. I got so used
to cockroaches droppin'

from the ceiling that even now
when I'm eatin', I cover up my food.
Hang 'em. Yes, sir. Hang 'em good.

2. Company Manual: Goals

*To teach basic vocational skills through on-the-job training
in an agricultural setting and to improve self-esteem through
a normalized work and living environment.*

3. Alford Busby

He's one of those people
you always call by their first

and last name no matter how long
you known him. Alford Busby.

Not just Alford. Not Busby.
Not Mr. Busby, that's for sure.

Alford Busby. He weren't afraid
to say no. *Alford Busby*, they say

to him, *go on to bed. Alford Busby,
turn off that TV*. Alford Busby

says *I ain't goin' to bed. Ima sit
right here and watch* Gunsmoke.

And Alford Busby would sit
on that itchy plaid sofa and plant

his feet on the floor so hard
the rats would go running

off to every corner of the room.
They says *Alright then,*

*Alford Busby, get your hands up
on the pole*, and they'd pull him up

by his big ol' arms
and make him hold that pole

for hours and hours. We'd eat
dinner and wash the dishes

and Alford Busby would still
be holdin' that pole like he was

keepin' the bunkhouse
from fallin' down on our heads.

One day it got to snowin' hard.
They tells Alford Busby *Time for bed,*

boy, and he gets mad, so mad.
Alford Busby says *That's it,*

and he walks out the door—
this was before they put the chains

on. He walks out in the snow
until he's gone. They looked

for him but Alford Busby
weren't nowhere

to be found. We whispered
'bout where he went, 'bout how

he musta made it to the ranch
they promised us we'd move to

when we retired. It has horses
runnin' free and a pond packed

so full of fish that your rod
never comes up empty.

They even say we can have
a dog, and I have in mind a sheltie

like the one I had back home
before I was sent away. Mitzi.

She liked to lick my face after I ate
buttered corn. It was spring

when they found Alford Busby.
Things was startin' to thaw

and a farmer on Wiggins Road
found him face down in his field

frozen solid, no boots
or coat. They made sure we

knowed about it, said *Don't you
be gettin' no ideas o' your own.*

We were all sad. Alford Busby
was 37 years old. Alford Busby

weren't afraid to say no.
Alford Busby was our hero.

4. Company Manual: Retention

*For most clients, a good adjustment is made and this is reflected in
the record of a low 15 percent turnover rate.*

5. Mrs. Avery

We called them *The Boys* even though
they were grown men, some older
than we were. They always seemed happy.
They came to the parades and town fair.
Those boys loved the dunking booth.
Harold Miner always made sure each of them
hit the target. How they'd laugh and laugh

when the platform collapsed and the bank president
or school principal went down with a splash!

They attended Sunday school, and even though
some of the hymns were a mouthful for them,
they hummed along as best they could.
We'd see them in the Mini-Mart counting out
pennies for honey buns and a cold pop,
and if they were short a nickel or a dime,
one of us would always slide a coin across
the counter. I mean, I'm sure the labor was hard,

but they seemed proud to earn their keep,
and what were the options, really, for the mentally re–,
mentally challenged? In the early days, they'd have
Christmas parties and open houses, and we would
sip punch and admire the evergreen garlands
they'd strung in the dining room. Back then,
they had a pool table and a gym and caretakers
who seemed nice. One of the boys could tap
out Jingle Bells with a plastic fork and spoon.

How were we to know things had gotten so bad?
When I read in the *Muscatine Journal* about
the rodents and mold, I said to my husband,
If you look up the word deplorable *in the dictionary,
this is what you'll find.* We felt sick with shame.
We called them *The Boys* and sometimes even
Our Boys. I want the world to know that we are
not to blame.

6. Company Manual: Recognition

*For his innovative work with mentally retarded men, company
co-founder T.H. Johnson received the coveted 'Employer of the Year'
award from the National Association for Retarded Citizens.*

7. Denise Gonzales

I thought I'd seen everything
a social worker could see:
children sleeping in dog crates,
seniors with bed sores the size

of saucers. But nothing could
prepare me for what I found
in that old schoolhouse: 21 men
with rotting teeth, toenails

so long they curled into the pads
of their feet like leeches.
And the smell: urine-soaked
mattresses, mouse feces, bodies

that hadn't been bathed
in weeks. Their forked hands
were covered in what looked like
a bad rash. We learned it was

dried blood. Turkey blood.
Yet still they reached out
to welcome me. *You the new
boss lady?* they asked.

8. Company Manual: Costs

Average client monthly income: $750.
Average client monthly expenses: $750.

9. Keith Brown

Some o' the others is in nursin' homes
now. Bobby and Billy Penner live
on their own up to Waterloo.

Ron and Johnny moved back
with family. Pete and Doyle is gone.
I got me an apartment in Arkansas.

I got a job and a cat. I like to watch
The Price is Right. I like the part
when they spin that big wheel.

I never miss a day of work. I never
eat no turkey. I never hurt another
bird 'cause I know how it feels.

Recall

> *I cannot tell you why it took years for a safety defect to be announced.* —Mary T. Barra, CEO of General Motors

Tungsten Arc. That's the kind of welding
he was studying in tech school. But I always

pictured his tongue—it was longer than most.
He liked to show the girls how he could stretch it

up to touch his nose like a copperhead.
They'd say *Eww, Daddy! Ewwww!* and then:

Again! Do it again! I'll admit we were careless.
We smoked weed. We drank. Weekends the girls

stayed at our place, we left a box of Cocoa Puffs
by their mattress so they could eat in the morning

without waking us up. I won't get any awards
for step-mothering—if you can even call it that

since we weren't hitched. The day of the accident,
I was taking him to pick up his car at a buddy's house.

We'd been there the night before watching
the game. The Colts killed us, 49-14.

Like most roads in east Texas, the highway is flat—
flat as the backside of a tombstone, my granddaddy

always said. Miles of tall grass and cows grazing
behind barbed wire. The sun was sitting high up

in the sky. There was a curve. A little curve.
And that's the last I remember. I've told the story

so many times it tells itself now. Those lawyers
dug up every bit of dirt they could find on us—

talked to his ex, to the neighbors, even tracked
down my high school teachers. It was my fault,

they said. People say something enough,
you start believing it's true. Here's all I know

for sure: when I came to, the car was smack up
against a tree, and he was laying across my lap

like he was sleeping. God knows how long
we'd been there. The blood on my arms was dry.

And I said *Baby, baby wake up. You're gonna be late
for class.* He was learning to be a welder so he could

get a job that paid better. He liked welding.
It was all about putting things back together.

Nothing to Trade

Finally we have nothing to trade, only a cough
and a skeleton nobody cares about.

—from the poem "Sleepless" by Xu Lizhi, a Chinese worker
who leapt to his death in September 2014 from a dormitory
run by his employer, an electronics manufacturing company
that produces most of the world's iPhones.

In Shenzhen, everything shines.
Mirrored windows of skyscrapers

glint like the scales of silver carp
men once caught in this seaside village.

Everything shines: silk costumes
of folk dancers who bow and twirl

for foreign tourists. The polished
marble floors of the Shajing mall,

sequined dresses of mannequins
frozen in shop displays. Imposing

gates that wall off corporate bosses'
families and luxury cars—and the sleek

sedans themselves, waxed and buffed
by drivers in dark, sparkling glasses.

Everything shines: tiny parts
on assembly lines, welding guns

that spray fireworks as if each day
is a celebration. Laminated badges

on managers who keep watch
from behind one-way glass, emerging

like birds in cuckoo clocks to bark
Faster, faster! Everything shines:

the bruised and burned limbs
of workers who earn a single break

during each 18-hour shift. The film
of chicken broth they sip standing up

before returning to their stations
early to avoid being fired or fined.

In Shenzhen, everything shines,
everything blinds.

HR Erasure: Policy on Manager Responsibilities

Violate your country

and principles

every day.

Learn that no one

expects you to be

good. Business must

always come first.

Avoid the appearance

of ethics.

Make sure

everyone gets hurt.

HR Erasure: Policy on Policy Statements

This   is   the   culture,

unwritten   for   there   are

no   words.   The   syntax

has   been   approved.   Avoid

pronouns   and   proper

names.   Limit   the   use

of   italics   and   bold.

Personal   information

must   be   removed.

On   the   line   below,

write   what   you   believe

you   have been   told.

HR Erasure: Policy on Clarity

Use   euphemisms.

        Be   ambiguous.

Choose   your   own   definitions

                for   words,

your   own   geography

        of   jargon.   Rightsize

                your   reality.

The   company   adjusts.

                The   company

                        seeks   feedback.

The   company   empowers.

        All   days   are   not

        days.   All   hours

are   not   hours.   All   hours

        are   not   ours.

McRant

Mike thinks he's all that 'cause he wears
a blue dress shirt and tie. I want to get right up
in his greasy face and say *You're nothing
but a McManager—get over yourself.*
But that'll land me on drive-thru duty all winter,
the fast food version of solitary confinement—
four hours in the freezing cold. Sure, they give you
a jacket, but it's so thin you can see through it.
Oh, and don't forget the fingerless gloves—
by the end of the shift, your fingertips
are so numb you could dip 'em in the deep fryer
and not feel the pain. Meanwhile, Mike yells
at us over every little thing: *I need more nuggets,
STAT!* he screams like he's a surgeon
saving lives. Of course he's sweet as pie
to the customers. This one lady spent
10 minutes making me describe every salad
in great detail, then ordered a chicken sandwich.
When I counted out her change, she wrinkled
up her face. *This nickel is dirty*, she says to me.
Dirty! Like every other coin she's ever touched
was sanitized and individually wrapped.
I want a clean nickel, she tells me. Well, I already
closed the register, so I have to get Mike to come over
and key in his secret override number that he protects
like it's the launch code for a nuclear bomb.
And do you know what he tells her? He says
*Oh yes, ma'am, you're right—that nickel is filthy.
Let's get you a new one*, and he digs around until he
finds the shiniest coin in the drawer. The lady
walks away and Mike turns to me with his supersized
sneer and says *Krista, do not let that happen again.*
I want to say *It's Trista, McAsshat. The least you
could do is learn my name.*

Ike Turner's Obituary

Tina
Tina
Tina

Shitshow

Shitshow should be one word
is a thought I've had at least

three times this week. Not
shit [stop] show as the dictionaries

and Autocorrect insist. What
do they know? Shit is not modifying

show—it is the show and the show
is shit: tarry dung, inexorable

excrement. Yesterday, for example,
we saw an elderly man try to exit—

I know, I know *disembark*—
a luxury sailboat. Unhinged on one side,

the sliver of dock became,
with each step, a horizontal see-saw,

the already unsteady man teetering
left right left. Those of us sipping

margaritas at the nearby tiki bar
gasped but didn't help. Collectively,

we did that thing where you faux lunge
with no intention of actually budging.

Sure, class was at play—a man
with a toy worth more than the homes

some of us were lucky enough
to almost own. *Not it, not it.*

Who among us didn't secretly want
to see this Thurston Howell III pitch

into the brackish bay below? Which
of us was the show, which the shit?

Elegy for the 30-Year Career

My mother's father, raised on a farm,
spent his working years at a helicopter plant.
He rose at 4 a.m., left home by 5 sharp.
His lunchbox looked like a metal barn.

Inside: two turkey sandwiches on rye
slathered with cranberry sauce,
a banana, and a Thermos of black coffee,
all packed by my grandmother

when she returned from second shift
at the factory. For thirty years
he drove back roads from Pascoag
across the Connecticut state line.

He had heart bypass surgery in his fifties
to fix the disease that killed
his twin. Insurance kicked in, nothing
out of pocket. He had three weeks'

paid vacation. One spring he used
his time off to build the wishing well
my grandmother had always wanted.
Most summers they visited us down South,

their silver Airstream camper a sideways
silo in front of our house. When he retired,
he had a pension, benefits, and more time
to watch *Judge Judy* and help motorists

who were stranded or lost. And when he died,
he left his wife a house, some savings,
and the memory of a man who never had
a bad word for his company or his boss.

In Human Resources

In Human Resources
the weather is always

fluorescent. There are no
flies, only files in Human

Resources. The plastic
ficus plant wilts

in Human Resources.
In Human Resources

the motivational poster
of Mount Everest

tilts to the right.
In Human Resources,

in Human Resources,
in Human Resources.

In Human Resources
a calendar on the wall

has no months or dates.
Do not bother to smile

for your photo ID
in Human Resources.

In Human Resources
no one has a face.

House as Found Poem: Demi-Sonnets
an abecedarian

Audience

Instead of texting myself the draft of a new poem,
I accidentally send it to the Comcast tech. *Nipple,*
colostrum, unbuttoned blouse, breast—it's a demi-
sonnet on nursing. Our TV's been glitchy all week
and goes black during a series finale. *Try resetting*
the modem, says the cable guy. No luck. So I reset
myself—like Auden, I learn to look at an empty sky.

Body of Work

The body shop was owned by a tanned couple
with hard bodies who gave us a convertible loaner
and an invite to *the bluest body of water you've ever seen.*
Turns out they were swingers. I had a toddler and a 9-to-5.
I could barely swing time off to haul my tired body
to a doctor. But that week—top down, bass throbbing
through the seat's hot leather skin—this body came alive.

Cento

I am the woman who copies—
an eye which wants the world,
no verb   no noun.
I imagine the paper as a body—
greenhouse of living ache.
I am the woman who copies.
Take this   this take.

Docupoetics

Farmer's Market, Eastern Shore of Maryland, summer 2021

Free parking, grain-free treats for dogs whose owners
browse free-range brown eggs. Last month scores
of documents were found in a nearby attic, dry rotted
and tattered. One offered $30 for the capture of
a Negro man named Amos with coarse trousers and scars
beneath both eyes. It's not enough that this street is now
emblazoned with the words *Black Lives Matter.*

Ekphrasis

When my parents split, he got the projector—she got
the slides. Now both are mine. On our living room wall
I meet my college-girl mother in black & white—swept-up
hair, unfiltered smile. *Shot through the lens of love,*
my husband assumes. Perhaps. But I know my father loved
gadgets—he was likely swooning over f-stops, shutter drag.
And here I am, unprepared for sole custody of their past.

Found Poem

Painters transformed a bungalow from gray to marigold,
then learned they'd painted the wrong home.
The crew loaded their truck and fled the scene.
After a gray day at desks the color of dust, the owners
smiled pulling into the drive, each assuming the other
had arranged this bright surprise. Sometimes
even a gray world gives you just what you need.

Gerund

When Mad Libs had blanks for gerunds instead of
dumbed-down -ing verbs, we caressed wood pulp paper
with pencils, then erased to play again and again, *stroking*
becoming *licking* becoming *sucking* becoming *fucking*,
you becoming a junior whose boyfriend dies cheating,
drowning after careening drunk into a flooded creek, the other
girl escaping, you learning to fall in love with the pain.

Haiku

5-7-5 sounds like the measurements
of Skipper, Barbie's sturdy younger sister.
She had high tops instead of heels,
tennis togs, skis. In one model, you twisted
an arm to make small breasts bud on her
rubber chest. She never got Ken, but she
got something better: bendable knees.

Iambic Pentameter

When your resting rate falls to 34 faint raps
on a distant door, the doctor buries a tiny box
in your chest. Bluetooth, he explains—
a computer in another city tracks your pace
through a mobile phone. Our grandson asks if you
can play music with your heart. At night
I press my head against this new metronome.

Juxtaposition

I couldn't get enough of interspecies friendships—
rabbits cuddled up with deer, an ostrich nuzzling a giraffe—
until I saw a Border Collie run minor league bases
with a literal monkey on his back, the dog hurtling
toward home, the capuchin bouncing in a tiny cowboy hat.
From my perch, I wanted not to want to play God
with small clinging creatures or big ones swinging bats.

Kinesthesia

If you find yourself stranded at sea for days—
plucked by a riptide, say, or flung overboard—
your only choice is to tread. Let your limbs
weave and unweave a thread, the back of your
head nestled into the small pillow of each wave.
It's almost biblical: this swept arm or kicked leg
begets the next until you're saved. Or dead.

Literary Criticism

A wicker furniture set spills on the freeway—
loveseats, tables, chairs. Most land upright,
a proper teatime scene in the middle
of I-70 west. An SUV stops to snag
an ottoman. Big rigs reduce the rest
to deconstructed twigs. Scavengers pick
through the wreckage to build their nests.

Metaphor

The night of the closest supermoon
in 70 years, I scrolled through Facebook
posts of friends' photos. Peter's was best:
the moon floated above a red barn
in Roaring Spring like an illuminated balloon
without a string. I'm ashamed to say how long
it took me to look outside at the real thing.

Near Rhyme

Identical twin brothers you knew in school—
one went to Yale, one joined a punk band.
Years later, one was crashing with friends
the summer you, too, were between lives.
You slept with him on a twin mattress
with no sheets—a one-night stand.
You never asked if he was Dave or Dan.

Onomatopoeia

A kid on my son's Little League team says
You write poems? I know how to spell onomatopoeia
(and does). I ask if he knows what it means.
Yeah, my uncle has a bad case of it. I picture a man
walking around like Adam West in *Batman: Bam! Pow!
Splat! Slosh!* Turns out he's confusing onomatopoeia
with alopecia, a condition that causes hair loss.

Process

What I love most about sunrise over the ocean
is not the sun itself but the way orange-pink light
glances off a gossamer of water before it seeps
into sand. I don't understand tides, something about
gravity and the pull of the moon, a choreographed
mystery. So reassuring, as if the planet has only
one conjunction: *and* and *and* and *and*.

Quatrain

I hear Coltrane, mainly the four-note baseline
over which he chants four syllables—*a love supreme*—
reserving the rest of his breath for the tenor sax, hurtling
and hurting through four movements of hum and tug
and mood. In four decades he surged from journeyman
to jazz despite the lure of dope and booze. Four decades,
just four. How much less most of us do with more.

Repetition

Every morning I look for it: the paraplegic squirrel
that army-crawls across my yard and skitters in rings
around the base of a red oak—tail and legs dragging
like a bridal veil. Slipped from the nest? Nicked by a car?
Simply nature off-script? In a ritual of wits, this critter
dodges a swooping Cooper's hawk to scoop up nuts,
onyx eyes bristling with grit. Every morning I look for it.

Second Person

I once read a poem about desire
to a man who desired me. Who can
blame him for assuming he was *you*?
Instead of speaking, he walked across
the room, lifted my hair, and kissed
the back of my neck—which was enough
to make me almost desire him, too.

Tercet

They dated, split for three decades, then married.
Traveled three continents. Renovated three homes,
one overlooking the confluence of a canal, river,
and bay. Spent sunsets watching three-story freighters
glide through the shipping lane. Welcomed three
grandkids, including my son. Found three shadows:
liver, pancreas, lung. Made three wishes, all the same.

Underground Art

Cicadas don't disappear for 17 years. What you hear is
a lifetime's labor, from rice-sized eggs sown in grooves
of bark to mites feeding on plant juice. So much tunneling
and shedding of former selves. They emerge a final
draft, fat as a man's thumb. The Latin root for *cicada*
is *cicada*: etymology and entomology, a winged pun.
Each offers a song from his own body's hollow drum.

Vocative

Dear Reader, I hate poems that begin
Dear Reader, a direct address that is
at once too intimate and too formal.
Dear Poet, call me by name, mention
the mole below my ribs, the tender place
Chaucer called our heartspoon. Poet,
say nothing at all or make me swoon.

White Space

The week our youngest leaves home, an albino
ruby-throated hummingbird hovers at our feeder, furious
brushstrokes of a painter without a palette, a blackjack
dealer's shuffled deck. Her tail feathers—*is she a she?*—
are a meringue of whipped air. Her wings are opera
fans fluttering in box seats, the brief life of a child's
snow angel before it disappears.   Was it ever there?

X-genre

Instead of hybrid, I see hy*bird*—the form itself
on the brink of flight, swaddle of narrative unspooling
skein by skein against the sky. The night our too-small son
was cut from me—tiny feathered thing—I mewed
for my husband in a white recovery room. The nurse
who brought the wrong man apologized. She did not
understand that any hand or wing would do.

Yawp

after Whitman, Rich, and Clifton

I too am undrowned and undrowning,
unparched despite thirst, unmapped and un-
unhinged. I too unread the book of myths
first—I too am unlearning. I too unsquish
my mighty hips from little petty places
as I unsound my barbaric yawp, pressing an
unshut ear to the seashell murmur of yearning.

Zeugma

for R. in our 36th year

At twenty-one, I fell in love with a man
twice my age. When I told my mother, she held
my hand but not her tongue, sternly predicting
doom. A pregnant stray cat soon claimed our hearts
and first shared home. We kept her and the runt
we named Zeugma, a term for yoking together
two things that don't belong as one.

Coda: Ars Poetica

Post-social distancing, we were easily taxed by too much
talking yet talked even more, our tongues unleashing
oceans of words, clogging the throats of coastal roads
with seaweed and sand. Remember the joke about
the boy who didn't speak for years, then complained about
burnt toast? We are all raising a child ghost in the dark
rooms of ourselves. In the silences we say the most.

Notes

Word Problems, Assisted Living, and Taxonomies
The poems in these collections are demi-sonnets, a seven-line poetic form created by Erin Murphy.

Ancilla
"Abridged" series: These erasure poems are comprised of words taken from the cited texts. The words are in order and have not been altered, with the exception of bracketed words, which have been added. The number of "erased" words between each selected word varies.

"Hand Mit Ringen": Wilhelm Rontgen discovered the x-ray in 1895. He and Anna were married forty-seven years until she died after a lengthy illness.

"Alma Mahler, Postnuptial": The epigraph is an excerpt from a 20-page letter Gustav wrote to Anna in 1901, the year before they married. The letter specified his expectations and demands for their marriage, including the provision that Anna discontinue her own career in composition.

"Kant's Manservant": Reinhold Bernhard Jachmann was Kant's former student and friend who wrote an early biography of Kant.

"Nietzsche's Sister": Elisabeth Förster-Nietzsche was the younger sister of Friedrich Nietzsche. They were close as children but grew apart after she married the fanatic anti-Semite Bernhard Förster.

"The Other Daughter": The speaker of this poem is Mary Wollstonecraft's first daughter, Fanny, who committed suicide at age 22. Wollstonecraft died following the birth of her second daughter, Mary, who went on to marry Percy Bysshe Shelley and to write *Frankenstein*. Among Wollstonecraft's writings is a collection of lessons on childcare, from which the italicized lines in this poem are taken.

"The Lost Letter": Aunt Lavinia Norcross cared for Emily at age 2, while Emily's mother recovered from the birth of her second daughter, Lavinia "Vinnie" Dickinson.

"Poe's Last Letter, Abridged": Maria "Muddy" Clemm was Poe's aunt and mother-in-law. This letter, written on Sept. 18, 1849, is one of two letters written on that date. It is unclear which of the two is actually Poe's final correspondence.

"Calamity Jane at the Dime Museum": "Calamity Jane" was a featured attraction at the Kohl & Middleton Dime Museum for six weeks in 1896.

"Emma Lazarus's Statue of Liberty Sonnet, Abridged": Lazarus's poem "The New Colossus" contains the famous lines "Give me your tired, your poor,/Your huddled masses yearning to breathe free . . . "

"Mother of Invention": Tesla's older brother, Dane [pronounced "Dahnay"], died after being thrown from a horse. Tesla is thought to have suffered from synesthesia.

"Facing Manet": Alexandre was a teenage boy who ran errands for Manet and posed for his painting "Boy with Cherries." He hanged himself in Manet's studio.

"To Nellie, with Love from the Letter E": The epigraph is from Brisbane's 1922 obituary for Cochrane. She was born Elizabeth Cochran but changed the spelling to "Cochrane" because she thought it seemed more sophisticated.

"Origen de Las Dos Fridas": Frida Kahlo's 1939 painting "Las Dos Fridas" ("The Two Fridas") is a self-portrait portraying herself with contrasting personalities. She traced the idea for the painting to her memory of her childhood imaginary friend.

"Postcards from Ghost Ranch": Chabot, who worked as a caretaker in exchange for room and board, was somewhat infatuated with O'Keeffe. In their nearly decade-long correspondence—much of which focused on home repairs—Chabot included occasional descriptions of the landscape. Many of the images in the poem are based on her images.

Assisted Living

"Assisted Living" features poems about the poet's late mother-in-law, Ann Palmer De Prospo (1914-2013), a concert pianist and former leader of the Major Bowes' All-Girl Band.

Human Resources

"Rana Plaza": A building housing five factories in Savar, Bangladesh collapsed on April 24, 2012, killing nearly one-third of the 3,600 textile workers.

The **"HR Erasure"** series poems are based on various human resources manuals.

"The Boys from Atalissa": As subcontractors of Hill Country Farms, a branch of Henry's Turkey Service, the men depicted in this poem were subjected to squalid living quarters, brutal working conditions, and verbal and physical abuse until social service agencies intervened in 2009. The case led to the largest jury verdict in EEOC history. Information from the "Company Manual" sections is from the "Hill Country Farms Program Description," November 1, 1980, known within the company as "The Magic of Simplicity." Some details in the poem were gathered from articles in *The New York Times* and *The Des Moines Register*.

The names in **"Indigo"** are from memorials to enslaved people at the Whitney Plantation in Wallace, Lousiana.

"Ike Turner's Obituary" is an erasure of an excerpt of the obituary for Ike Turner published in *The New York Times* on Dec. 13, 2007.

House as Found Poem
"**Cento**": Credits (in order of appearance): Marilyn Hacker, Miriam Goodman, Marie Howe, Max Ritvo, Marianne Boruch, Rita Dove.

Acknowledgments

Thank you to the following organizations for their support: the Pennsylvania Council on the Arts, the Maryland State Arts Council, the Virginia Center for Creative Arts, the Pennsylvania Center for the Book, the Emma Barrientos Mexican American Cultural Center, the Whitney Plantation, the International Center for Photography, the Dorset Colony, the Penn State Altoona Advisory Board, the Humanities Institute (formerly the Institute for Arts and Humanities) at Penn State University, and the Mellon Foundation.

Science of Desire, a Paterson Poetry Prize finalist, was published by Word Poetry in 2004. Poems originally appeared in *The Georgia Review*, *America*, *The Lucid Stone*, *Dogwood Journal of Poetry & Prose*, *Literal Latte*, *Field*, *Red River Review* (Pushcart Prize nomination), and *Yankee* magazine. Awards: "ZipCodeMan" won the Writers' Union Poetry Award judged by Donald Hall. "Not Yet Named" received 2nd Place, *Literal Latte* Poetry Awards. "Elegy" received Honorable Mention in the *Yankee* Poetry Awards. "Studies" was reprinted in the anthology *Forgetting Home: Poems About Alzheimer's*. "Better Than Sex" was reprinted in the anthology *It's All Good*. "Birthday Poem" was reprinted in *180 More Extraordinary Poems for Every Day* edited by Billy Collins.

Dislocation and Other Theories, winner of the Paterson Award for Literary Excellence, was published by Word Poetry in 2008. Poems originally appeared in *America*, *North American Review*, *Nimrod International Journal of Poetry & Prose*, *Flash*, *Southeast Review*, *Red River Review*, *Listening to Water: The Susquehanna Rivershed Anthology*, *Bat Creek Review*, *The Broadkill Review*, *Paterson Literary Review*, and *Oberon*. Awards: "Covetous" received the 2006 Foley Poetry Award. "Inter-" received a 2006 Dorothy Sargent Rosenberg Poetry Prize. "Hula Dancer" was reprinted in *The Flash* anthology (London) and *Fantastic Imaginary Creatures: An Anthology of Contemporary Prose Poems*. "Covetous" was reprinted in *Making Poems: 40 Poems with Commentary by the Poets*.

"Amphibious" was featured on NPR's *The Writer's Almanac* hosted by Garrison Keillor.

Too Much of This World, winner of the Anthony Piccione Poetry Prize, was published by Mammoth Books in 2008. Special thanks to the late Tony Vallone, publisher. Poems originally appeared in *Field*, *Green Mountains Review*, and *Paterson Literary Review*. Awards: "Debriefing: a Poem in Parts" won the Normal School Poetry Prize judged by Nick Flynn and was nominated for a Pushcart Prize. "Does This Poem Make My Butt Look Big?" was reprinted in *Nasty Women Poets: An Unapologetic Anthology of Subversive Verse*.

Word Problems, winner of the Paterson Award for Literary Excellence, was published by Word Poetry in 2011. Poems originally appeared in *Southern Women's Review*, *Boston Literary Magazine*, *Taj Mahal Review*, *Tattoo Highway*, *Scythe Literary Journal*, *Yale Journal for Humanities in Medicine*, *The Summerset Review*, *subterrain*, *Arbor Vitae*, *Kestrel*, and *Los Angeles Review*. Awards: "Sea Shells" was selected by judge Patricia Smith for inclusion in the 2009 *Best of the Net* anthology.

Distant Glitter, a Foreword INDIES Book of the Year finalist, was published by Word Poetry in 2013. Poems originally appeared in *The Normal School*, *subtropics*, *Connotations*, *Delaware Poetry Review*, *Shakespeare's Monkey Review*, *Literary Mama*, *Etchings*, *The Summerset Review*, and *Fledgling Rag*. Awards: "Vow" was selected for the Pennsylvania Center for the Book's Poetry Award and nominated for a Pushcart Prize.

Ancilla, winner of the Fred Allen Womack and Frances Sue Zimmerman Womack Book Award, was published by Lamar University Press in 2014. Poems originally appeared in *North American Review*, *Southern Indiana Review*, *Nimrod International Journal*, *Kalliope*, *Atlanta Review*, *The Blue Max Review*, *Beltway*, and *Dislocate*. Awards: "Mother of Invention" won the Fermoy (Ireland) International Poetry Prize.

Assisted Living, winner of the Brick Road Poetry Prize, was published by Brick Road Poetry Press in 2018. Poems originally appeared in *Barrelhouse, Rise Up Review, The Summerset Review, Review Americana, Qarrtsiluni,* and *Blackwater.* Some selections appeared in the chapbook *Remorse Code* published in the Seven Kitchens Press Keystone Chapbook Series. "Fall, Central Pennsylvania" was reprinted in the anthology *Keystone Poetry.*

Taxonomies was published by Word Poetry in 2022. Poems originally appeared in *The Laurel Review, Contrary, Quartet, MacQueen's Quinterly, Artemis, Shot Glass Journal, DASH, Résonance, Alba, NOON: journal of the short poem,* and *The Citron Review.* "Taxonomies of Rasps" was reprinted in *White Winged Doves: A Stevie Nicks Poetry Anthology.* "Taxonomy of Menopause" was reprinted in the anthology *Rising from the Ashes.*

Fluent in Blue, winner of the American Book Fest Best Book Award in Poetry, was published by Grayson Books in 2024. Poems originally appeared in *Poet Lore, North American Review, Waxwing, Rattle, Passages North, Diode, Narrative Northeast, Jellyfish Review, SWWIM, Brevity* podcast, *Unbroken, ONE ART: a journal of poetry, Literary Mama, The Summerset Review, MER, North American Review,* and *About Place.* "Hide-and-Seek" was reprinted in *The Strategic Poet.* Awards: "The Internet of Things" was the winner of the 2021 Rattle Poetry Prize Readers' Choice Award; "Vaughn" was nominated for a Best of the Net Award; "Anthimeria" and "Azul" were finalists for the James Hearst Poetry Prize from the *North American Review.*

Human Resources was published by Grayson Books in 2025. Poems originally appeared in *Women's Studies Quarterly, Southern Humanities Review, North American Review, Glass, Rabbit* (Australia), *Scoundrel Time, Arkana, The Summerset Review,* and *Action, Spectacle!* Awards: "McRant" was nominated for a Pushcart Prize.

House as Found Poem is new work. Poems originally appeared in *Ecotone, Dialogist, Writers Resist, Rogue Agent, Rattle, RockPaperPoem, Eastern Iowa Review, Elysium Review, MacQueen's Quinterly, ONE ART: a journal of poetry, The New Verse News, Northern Appalachia Review, Variant Literature, Painted Pebble, Molecule, Just YA: Short Poems, Essays, and Fiction for Grades 7-12,* and *In a Nutshell: An Anthology of Short Poems.*

These poems and my life as I know it would not be possible without the love and support of Rich, Molly, Nathan, Rebecca, Amy, Sam, Adam, Erica, Collin, Joanna, Donna, Patti, Lauren, John, Shawn, Pete, Anthony, and Kara, as well as those who have moved on from this life: Viola, Chris, Ann, James, Madelin, Dickie, and David K.

About the Author

Erin Murphy is the author or editor of more than a dozen previous books of poetry and prose, most recently *Mother as Conjunction: Lyric Essays*, *Human Resources*, and *Fluent in Blue*, winner of the 2025 American Book Fest Best Book Award in Poetry. Her edited anthologies of poetry, creative nonfiction, medical humanities, and docupoetics are published by Wesleyan University Press, the University of Nebraska Press, and SUNY Press.

She received her M.F.A. in Poetry from UMass Amherst where she wrote her thesis under the direction of James Tate. Her work has appeared in *Ecotone*, *The Georgia Review*, *Women's Studies Quarterly*, *Southern Humanities Review*, *Rattle*, *The Best of Brevity*, *Best Microfiction*, *Best of the Net*, and anthologies from Random House, Bloomsbury, and Bedford/St. Martin's.

Her awards include a Dorothy Sargent Rosenberg Poetry Prize, two Foreword INDIES Book of the Year awards, the National Writers Union Poetry Prize judged by Donald Hall, the Foley Poetry Award, and the Patterson Prize for Literary Excellence.

She serves as poetry editor of *The Summerset Review* and has spearheaded numerous interdisciplinary projects, including "Life Lines," an initiative that pairs students in the social sciences with senior citizens for poetry-writing experiences. In keeping with her commitment to making poetry accessible to all, two of her books are available free online: *The Book of Jobs: Poems About Work* and *Fields of Ache: Centos*. Murphy is professor of English at Penn State Altoona and the 2026-27 Penn State Laureate.

Website: www.erin-murphy.com